Architecture
Transformed

Architecture Transformed

Hubert Locher
Dominik Lengyel
Florian Henrich
Catherine Toulouse

The Digital Image
in Architecture
1980–2020

Birkhäuser
Basel

Table of Contents

Hubert Locher,
Dominik Lengyel,
Florian Henrich,
Catherine Toulouse

Architecture
Transformed

1   The DFG Priority Program "The Digital Image" website, <https://www.digitalesbild.gwi.uni-muenchen.de/das-digitale-bild/> (last accessed 31.1.2024). See *International Journal for Digital Art History*, 2021, 8 (Oct.): "The Digital Image" <https://journals.ub.uni-heidelberg.de/index.php/dah/issue/view/5810> (last accessed 31.1.2024).

2   See Hubert Locher, Dominik Lengyel, Catherine Toulouse, and Florian Henrich, "Architecture Transformed: Architectural Processes in the Digital Image Space," in *The Digital Image* 2021, pp. 66–81.

This book emerged from the research project "Architecture Transformed—Architectural Processes in the Digital Image Space," which was undertaken from 2019 to 2022 in cooperation with the Deutsches Dokumentationszentrum für Kunstgeschichte—Bildarchiv Foto Marburg (German Documentation Center for Art History—Bildarchiv Foto Marburg) and the Lehrstuhl für Architektur und Visualisierung der Brandenburgischen Technischen Universität Cottbus-Senftenberg (Chair of Architecture and Visualization at the Brandenburg University of Technology (BTU) Cottbus-Senftenberg). It is one of the subprojects forming part of the Deutsche Forschungsgemeinschaft (DFG, German Research Foundation) priority program 2172 "The Digital Image." The priority program (SSP) is coordinated by Hubertus Kohle (Munich) and Hubert Locher (Marburg) in two consecutive three-year phases from 2020 to 2026. It examines "the central role played by the image in the complex process of digitizing knowledge, both in theory and in practice" from different perspectives in a series of exemplary projects across the whole of Germany and reflects on the associated ongoing transformation in art, science, and culture as a "profound epistemological upheaval."[1]

The project "Architecture Transformed" focuses on examples showing the role of the digital image in the field of architecture. It is one of those projects within the scope of the priority program that are based on a combination of two practical research approaches that differ clearly from each other in relation to the object under consideration and are therefore complementary. The first takes an art-historical perspective from the viewpoint of the "history and theory of image media," while the second engages architecturally with the examples with particular reference to the question of design conception and the practical realization of architectural visualizations.

At the heart of the project is the question of the influence of the digital image on architectural designs and visualizations in the transition from the analog to the digital age and specifically the extent to which the use of digital design and representation methods may result in a media-specific shaping of the architecture.[2] The production and concept of architecture, we assume, are not only shaped by their technical and constructional aspects but also by their visual representation. Building design involves a number of different artistic processes. From the first conception in hand-drawn sketches to the fleshed-out presentation in the competition and the design visualization for the purpose of reflection, communication, and marketing, architects have always used methods of visual modeling and pictorial representation—from drawings and physical models to photography. Architecture appears from this perspective as a complex process undertaken by different actors, as a process intended to end with a built artifact, but one that exists in media form developed from a thought or idea before it becomes a material object. Architecture, as a sensually perceivable and practical three-dimensional structure containing space, is the physical result, the material reference object, in which what was previously developed and negotiated in a complex, sometimes protracted, iterative design process manifests itself.

Visualization plays a central role in this process. On one hand, the thoughts and ideas behind the architecture require illustration. On the other hand, these ideas have already been shaped by other, previously

Architecture Transformed

3   Beatriz Colomina, *Privacy and Publicity: Modern Architecture as Mass Media*, Cambridge (Mass.) 1994.

4   Cervin Robinson and Joel Herschman (ed.), *Architecture Transformed: A History of the Photography of Buildings from 1839 to the Present*, Cambridge (Mass.) 1987.

assimilated images, no matter whether they be images of completed buildings, visualizations of architecture that has not yet been built, or images that appear to have nothing to do with architecture. Even the realized building, which must be visited for its specific architectural qualities to be experienced, will from then on be judged in the form of images, whether that be in professional journals, in lifestyle magazines, in architectural historiography, or in the digital channels of social media. Architecture, as a vague idea, as a presented design, or as a physical object, has always to rely on images in order to be communicated through media. Against this background, architectural representations cannot be viewed as merely incidental or negligible; they are much more an integral component of what eventually appears as architecture.

Deep-seated changes come about during the 1980s when digital technologies for the design and visual representation of architecture (computer-aided design, computer rendering) are becoming established, bringing with them completely new opportunities for linking technical design and pictorial reproduction. Designers can now use digital methods to continually create visualizations, different perspectives, and effective formulations of appearances for a wide range of purposes and occasions. By this time, realistic representations can be created in the early phases of a design. With powerful modern computers opening the way for new structures, not only is the generation of free-form shapes determined from their appearance and not from elementary tectonic considerations brought to the fore but also the type of forms generated can actually be translated into built architecture.

The question of what consequences and effects for the architectural design of the present are particularly linked with the digital image arises increasingly frequently. However, instead of simply making a sweeping assumption that form is determined by the digital tools, we have attempted to explore the essential connection between design and visualization, between the production and representation of architecture. Such a connection may have generally existed ever since there have been pictorial representations of architecture, but the relationship has gained significance with the availability of what might be called technical reproduction media, which Beatriz Colomina brought out in exemplary fashion in 1994 for the relationship of architecture, photography, and mass media since the beginning of the twentieth century.[3] In this sense, Cervin Robinson and Joel Herschman had already pointed out some years before in their publication *Architecture Transformed: A History of the Photography of Buildings from 1839 to the Present*[4]—upon which we drew for the title of our project—that the idea or the concept of architecture changes, depending on the manner and means of its representation. Architectural photographs lead those who study them to other imagined images of architecture than, for example, drawings; and, like the drawing representation, the photographic representation of architecture is also linked with media transformations that shape the represented object in specific ways. However these media forms are created, they have one thing in common: they differ significantly from how architecture is experienced directly.

This is the starting point for the research project on the digital image in architecture. We believe we can establish that a renewed, profound media reshaping of the architectural in the character of the

Hubert Locher, Dominik Lengyel, Florian Henrich, Catherine Toulouse

5 Teresa Fankhänel and Andres Lepik (ed.), *The Architecture Machine: The Role of Computers in Architecture*, exhib. cat. Munich, Basel 2020.

6 Hubert Locher, Dominik Lengyel, Florian Henrich, and Catherine Toulouse (ed.), *Architecture Transformed—Das digitale Bild in der Architektur 1980–2020*, exhib. cat., Heidelberg 2023. DOI: https://doi.org/10.11588/arthistoricum.1156

7 Hubert Locher, Dominik Lengyel, Florian Henrich, and Catherine Toulouse (ed.), *Rendering / Visualisierung* (Begriffe des digitalen Bildes, 5), Munich 2024. DOI: https://doi.org/10.5282/ubm/epub.109214

pictorial takes place in the course of digitalization. This transition from analog to digital and its consequences for the practice need to be reflected also in architecture, as the recently held exhibition *The Architecture Machine* at the Technical University Munich (TUM) made clear.[5] Perhaps more than ever before, architecture, individual buildings, or designs are perceived, mediated, and present in the form of images, worldwide and simultaneously. And just as photographic reproductions in books and journals were once a source of stimulation, today digital representations are helping to shape the architectural discourse; in other words, they play a role in the conversation about architecture and influence those who themselves design and visualize architecture.

While the Cottbus subproject deals with the operative aspect of the image as a visual component of digital design tools and analyzes the effects of CAD software on the results achieved with them, the Marburg subproject traces the development of the digital image in the mirror of architectural journals from 1980 to the present day while taking into consideration the accompanying contemporary discussion. The role of the digital image as a communicative medium between architectural mediation and marketing is likewise subjected to critical reflection. The findings of the project are brought together in a subjective selection of fifty-one architectural images that were taken from the studied journals or from the material submitted for the Schinkel architectural design ideas competition. The project attempts to trace the development of the digital image as a medium for architectural representation in the last four decades under the influence of digitalization by means of significant representative examples. These exemplary images, together with the descriptive, analytical, and explanatory texts in chronological order, form the core of this book.

The main findings of this research were presented in an exhibition held in three locations in Germany during 2023: the Museum of Art at the Philipps University Marburg, the Architectural Museum of the Technical University of Berlin (TU Berlin), and the Information, Communication and Media Center (IKMZ) of the Brandenburg University of Technology Cottbus-Senftenberg (BTU). A publication accompanying the exhibition was made available in German.[6] Other findings of this research have been published in a volume of the priority program (SSP) brochure series "Concepts of the digital image."[7] With this book, the material can now also be presented in English.

We would like to thank all the participating architectural offices and people for their readiness to collaborate with us on the exhibition, for their information, for making available the image files and granting the image rights. The Deutsche Forschungsgemeinschaft (German Research Foundation (DFG)) made the research work possible by funding the project, publication was supported by the Deutsches Dokumentationszentrum für Kunstgeschichte—Bildarchiv Foto Marburg (German Documentation Center for Art History (DDK)—Bildarchiv Foto Marburg), and the Philipps University Marburg. We are grateful to the schneider+schumacher architectural practice in Frankfurt am Main for its donation. Last but not least, we would like to thank Birkhäuser Verlag as the publisher and particularly Katharina Holas for inclusion in the publishing program.

9

Dominik Lengyel,
Catherine Toulouse

The Production Process for the Digital Image in Architecture

1   This applies equally to the retrospective digital image. In the chapter "New Media for the Visualization of Architecture," we describe how the digital image can be an effective research instrument beyond architecture and within the sphere of historical natural sciences and humanities, above all in archaeology: Dominik Lengyel and Catherine Toulouse, "New Media for the Visualization of Architecture," in *New Media in Art History: Tensions, Exchanges, Situations*, ed. Régine Bonnefoit, Melissa Rérat, and Samuel Schellenberg, Berlin and Boston 2023, pp. 116–31.

2   This form of teaching of visualization as architectural design in the image is a permanent component of our foundation course in the bachelor's degree program in architecture. One book describes some examples of student work: Dominik Lengyel and Catherine Toulouse (ed.), *Perspektiven gestalten: Studienarbeiten des ersten Studienjahres*, BTU Brandenburg University of Technology Cottbus, 2008.

The unlimited possibilities of use for the computer and its ever-wider scope of application also have the consequence that the understanding of its role continues to vary very significantly. Artificial intelligence is used in the widest sense not only for the analysis of digital images but also increasingly for the synthesis of them. This was responsible in a special way for the vehemence surrounding digital images as well as their acceptance or rejection, above all in the architectural community, around the time of the change of millennia. We therefore see it as important for research on the digital image in architecture to explain the production process and its perhaps crucial added value, namely the ability to verify these images using digital models.[1]

For the production of a digital architectural image, if purely image compilation techniques such as collages are not used, a three-dimensional model is generally first built then projected using rendering algorithms and post-processed into a digital image. The projection imposes the first special characteristic: the model must contain nothing more than those elements that are directly or indirectly visible in the final image. Also contrary to what the image suggests, the model may consist only of a backdrop. The result of the computer process, which is the actual rendering, is then post-processed using specialist software such as Photoshop, which has set the standard for many decades due to its wide range of functions and possibilities. This operation mainly involves correction and adjustment of the image tone, brightness, color, and color temperature but may also include methods used in traditional photomontages. Photomontage can also mean the insertion of rendering into the architectural context as well as the reverse process of placing elements such as people, vehicles, or vegetation into the rendering.

As is the case with every projection, even of haptic models, it is not difficult to misrepresent the spaces in the digital model. A very common method is the removal of walls to achieve a greater viewing distance within the internal spaces. The greater distance to the virtual camera then creates a perspective image with a larger area of internal space and less edge distortion. The subjective impression of space can thus be made to look more realistic, but this projection is impossible to achieve geometrically in the built architecture (without tearing down the walls). Such possibilities to misrepresent are no easier, more frequent, or more of a natural thing to do than with analog images. With digital images, however, people almost automatically assume they are geometrically correct, because digital images suggest a higher commitment to geometric accuracy through a supposed or simply a clearly recognizable desire for realism. The reputational damage to the digital image based on its presumed easy corruptibility is certainly unjust, but it is clear, when in fact exactly the reverse could be true. Such a digital image is geometrically verifiable simply by directly connecting the digital image to the underlying digital model.

In order to be able to trace the creation of a digital image, we consider its production not only as a technical process but also and primarily as a creative process. The rest of this chapter sets out to explain, based on a student seminar, our part in the subproject about the digital image in architecture in the priority program "The Digital Image."[2] It seeks to examine the central question of the project: To what extent does the digital tool—in this case the customized specialist CAD

11

Fig. 1

software—influence the process of design and visualization and therefore the built architecture?

To approach this question empirically, it was originally planned to work with old software running in an emulator to be able to observe the influence of two quite different program types that stand in stark contrast to one another, especially in their first versions. The umbrella term "Computer-Aided Design," or CAD, falls short of describing the huge differences these tools made, particularly in the early phase of the software. This is also clear in the images of buildings published in the architectural journals collected and evaluated as part of the research project. Thanks to the pandemic, when it came to conducting the study, the students had to dispense with using the prepared old versions at the university and instead fall back on the then-current versions of the software on their own personal computers.

Those taking part in the seminar were asked to design a refuge for two people on the proverbial greenfield site. No stipulations were made for the architectural design. With these rules, we wanted to bring about a maximum of intrinsic design while guaranteeing a high level of comparability.

The participants could choose between two CAD programs, ArchiCAD and Rhinoceros, which, at the time of their appearance, were diametrically conceived. ArchiCAD had set out to revolutionize the design of architecture by having exclusively defined components that could be placed in space—in other words, objects implemented to function as specific components. A wall was a wall and remained so, a roof was a roof, and so on. On the other hand, Rhinoceros is something more like technical drawing according to the rules of descriptive geometry, albeit in space. The geometric possibilities generally exceed the needs of architecture, provided that the architecture is not like the shapes found in automotive design. More than sixty second-year students on the bachelor's degree course participated as part of a compulsory module and this exercise was worth three credit points.

In architectural design in perspective, which is studied in this seminar using examples, representation and design continually influence one another, and having one without the other is inconceivable. Design in perspective—and not in plan—sets the design directly in the spatial context. Above all, however, designing in perspective anticipates the perception of the eventual users and thus—something that is a central epistemic objective—avoids surprises.

The immanent evaluation is the crucial difference from design in plan. It shows, time and time again, that significant changes in the perspective do not show themselves at all in plan. This does not make the plan and other typically planimetric projections, such as elevation and section, any less important, and certainly not at all for construction. However, they are not sufficient on their own for the totality of the architectural design.

Fig. 1 shows how much the effect of an image can change while the basic idea changes little. The last version in the series, especially, is interwoven more clearly within the image. This applies also to the further-developed connection between internal and external space, but above all to the lighting, which allows the rendering to appear plausible as a building standing in the photograph.

Dominik Lengyel, Catherine Toulouse

Fig. 2

By designing in perspective, the author of this work soon recognized that a formal idea is not powerful enough on its own. The next steps therefore show how she develops an architecturally realizable shelter and abandons the original motif. The final step is to develop those elements that have successfully emerged from the selection process. The progress of the work over the semester shows how designing in perspective can initiate a cycle of reflection.

A three-dimensional idea also starts the design process in Fig. 2. But this one proves more durable than that of the work in Fig. 1. It is therefore retained and fleshed out step by step. The importance of the perspective for the design process is also evident here. The effect of the rod-shaped elements at different orientations and points in space would disappear in a planimetric projection. Only in the side elevation would any sign of the form of two inclined elements be apparent. In the perspective view, on the other hand, the formal principle remains recognizable and effective, right down to the furnishings.

The study, which was the focal point in this seminar, was aimed at differentiating the influences of the different design concepts of the two CAD programs, which today are identified by two acronyms seeking to express the essence of the structure in completely different ways. The first genre is called Building Information Modeling (BIM), in which the metadata about the function of the object remains with the object, while the second genre directly adopts the mathematical function Non-Uniform Rational B-Spline (NURBS) as its name, which is the basis for the mathematics of complex surfaces. The latter is certainly a major difference compared with ordinary BIM programs, but in the end it depicts just one of many surface descriptions and finds use in only a few of the designs presented here.

BIM programs are particularly suitable in architectural practice for architects who work with other construction professionals, engineers, and urban planners. BIM allows integrated planning in which every piece of geometry has a direct functional attribute and is therefore handled as a functional component of the building.

NURBS programs, which were originally used in mechanical engineering and industrial design, model an object with geometrical precision, while allowing the highest number of possible degrees of freedom. Initially, objects remain purely geometrical objects without function, a cuboid remains a cuboid, a surface is infinitely thin and cannot be realized in a structure in this form. This freedom also means that the program does not permit the association of meaningful attributes to these objects. Association cannot take place until later.

The difference lies therefore not only in the usability of the three-dimensional model for rapid prototyping (for example 3D printing) or the exchange of design information with other construction professionals (such as air-conditioning engineers) but also in the inertia of the formal design process. The association of attributes to each and every component—according to our hypothesis—limits creativity because free modeling either disappears entirely or at least is considerably restricted. This is also clearly shown in the two seminar contributions in Fig. 3. Although NURBS has not been used, because practically all the elements are cuboid in both cases, objects are modeled intuitively more

The Production Process for the Digital Image in Architecture

3   How working with the computer as a whole is integrated in teaching the visualization of architecture is explained in: Dominik Lengyel and Catherine Toulouse, "Visualisierung in der Architekturlehre," in *Vom Baumeister zum Master. Formen der Architekturlehre vom 19. bis ins 21. Jahrhundert*, ed. Carola Ebert, Eva Maria Froschauer, and Christiane Salge (Forum Architekturwissenschaft, 3), Berlin 2019, pp. 256–85.

in detail without component references. How the modeling is done is described below.

BIM excels with prefabricated components because the function of the component has already been registered, which means the designer does not have to go through the time-consuming step of defining it. Simple components, such as walls and ceilings, can be defined easily by their outlines, but windows and doors are treated in the same way as furniture because of their geometrical complexity; they are entered as a complete unit into the library [Fig. 4a]. With free modeling, on the other hand, all the elements float freely in 3D space, and the designer places geometric elements there as required [Fig. 4b].

While modeling is the first technical step on the way to a digital image, the first creative step is, hopefully, the design idea. One of the serious difficulties in the acceptance of digital images in the early phase of CAD was that the technical capabilities of CAD had been given so much publicity that the design idea was willingly overlooked or simply skipped. Therefore, right at the beginning of the study project, it is important to conduct the design process outside the CAD environment and become aware of the influence of the CAD tool on the process and the resulting design.

The geometric structure that typically results from free modeling can be seen in the next design step. Window frames are not prefabricated components taken from a manufacturer's catalog, but rather a string of simple cuboids that give only the visual impression of window frames due to their dimensions [Fig. 5]. The concept of architecture is, however, more than the visible object alone. In contrast to the case in product design, the architectural object is tied to its place. This concept is not an inherent feature in CAD. The design possibilities in CAD are practically unlimited; everything can be represented geometrically— particularly with NURBS modeling—and designed. However, for the digital image of architecture as we understand it, for the visual communication of an architectural idea, there is no architectural context, no genius loci. Embedding geometry into the context can, as shown here, be done in the form of a photomontage.

Embedding geometry into a photograph is a less trivial task than it appears. The following images show not only the necessary steps by way of example using Photoshop (the leading image editing software), but also—which is particularly helpful in teaching—the most common errors.[3]

Generally, the photomontage is only the third stage in the whole design process of the digital image. The second stage is normally the rendering, which is the textured projection of the previously created virtual model. This applies mainly to the technical description of the creation process. However, the deeper sense specifically of designing in perspective is the mutual influence of these first three steps: model, rendering, montage. For example, it makes complete sense to carry out the materializing, that is to say the texturing of the model, beforehand on the photograph.

In the ideal case, the rendering process—and this is a main objective in the teaching of designing in perspective—cognitively anticipates the photomontage. Viewed purely in technical terms, the rendering process remains an independent intermediate step.

Fig. 3

14

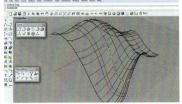

Fig. 4a, b

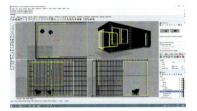

Fig. 5

The photomontage is produced semiautomatically. As well as creating the actual external appearance of the textured object, the rendering software adds what is generally referred to as a transparency channel, which gives a degree of opacity and uses the contours of the object as the border between the interior and the exterior of the object for a covering surface that, like a paper-cut artwork, portrays the object here, for example, in white and the background in black. Hence, the montage is almost automated at least as far as the edges of the object, but not so with the application of suitable textures and light [Fig. 6].

The digital model, however, cannot anticipate all the situations of the photomontage, because the difficulties of creating the digital image are not limited to the interfaces, and only the photomontage itself solves the problem.

The following comparison is intended to show what, apart from the contours, must be paid attention to in the production of digital images, where most mistakes occur, and how a catalog of criteria for evaluating them can be made. The most important criterion for photomontage is integrity. It relates to the plausible connection of rendering and photograph.

One of the most common errors, and one of the greatest difficulties when integrating a rendering into a photo, is the actual interface where they join, the simulated physical contact of the rendered content with the photographic content, generally the transition to the ground, and especially the transition to amorphous surfaces such as areas of grass [Fig. 7].

Other difficulties are shared with the analog photomontage. If, for example, the building inserted into the photograph is too small, it will not create the effect of a building; it will look like a photograph of an architectural model [Fig. 8]. The mistake would be easy to rectify by moving the building so that it looks closer to the position of the camera in the photograph. With reference to the photomontage, this means that the rendering would have to be moved downward on the photograph.

This simple measure would solve only the scale problem and not necessarily the orientation and, more importantly, the relative angle of tilt of the two components in the image. It can very quickly look as if the building is standing on sloping ground or one side of it has sunk into the earth.

Likewise, it could also be, to a limited extent, due to the focal length. The focal length is responsible for perspective effects, in other words the distortion of the building. In a photomontage, a wrong focal length is an objective error because it can clearly contradict the photograph [Fig. 9]. This problem would also be solvable by magnifying the render on the photo, which is the equivalent of reducing the distance to the physical camera and makes the building appear nearer. On the other hand, this could cause the building to appear too large, which would reintroduce the previously discussed problem of scale.

Other effects can occur due to the height of the virtual camera. In a montage, virtual and photographic horizons must agree, or else the building appears to tilt [Fig. 10]. Correcting the perspective as explained above is also possible here, by appropriately scaling the rendering: in Fig. 10a it is larger and in Fig. 10b smaller. However, here as well, the two renders would introduce the scale problem again.

15

Fig. 6 a–d

Another phenomenon, which may occur due to the same reason in either an analog photograph or an analog photomontage, is capable of correction in a different way and affects the visualization of the architecture quite significantly in most cases. It concerns the exact horizontal alignment of the viewing direction. Only when the viewing direction is precisely horizontal—the straight perspective that is nearest to what is naturally seen and causes no additional or intentional distortion—is the plane of the image exactly horizontal. Only in this case, according to the rules of geometry and photography without special lenses, do vertical building edges also look vertical in the image. Otherwise, it is difficult to say without further information whether the architecture is intended to be the way it looks, or whether the building actually has non-vertical surfaces, especially if walls are deliberately inclined, for example in fortifications. Fig. 11a shows the perspective projection of a building in which the building edges are vertical in three-dimensional space but appear tilted by the inclined image plane, while the image plane in Fig. 11b is vertical and therefore much closer to spatial perception.

Finally, the light is also a component of the digital image. Light shows not only that there is something there to see; it is also always crucial for the atmosphere, in other words the intended mood of the image. It is very seldom used to create a natural simulation. Fig. 12a shows the lightening of a nighttime internal space in a light-colored external skin. That would already look surreal even without the photomontage. In a photomontage, however, the error, combined with the contrast from sunlight shining from one side, is particularly noticeable. In Fig. 12b, on the other hand, the light of the photograph is correctly adjusted in the rendering. But it is not only the unambiguous direction of the light that determines the success of the integration of the rendering; there is also the adjustment of the textures by adapting the surface of the rendered geometry to the colors of light in the photograph. Here as well, the results show that rendering is not necessarily simply the first step in the production of the digital image; it is a multistage process that will naturally run more linearly with increasing experience. Fig. 13a shows a strangely colored object, while the colors from the rendering and photograph in Fig. 13b are much closer to one another. Perhaps the most frequently encountered error in the production of digital images is the use of repetitive textures, as shown in Fig. 14a. It is difficult to say why this error is so persistent. One possible reason is that, at least to the untrained eye, textures effectively obscure the simplified geometry. This is the way the early three-dimensional computer games worked, around the same time as the first digital images in architecture included in this research project. In our teaching, we work consistently and with great energy to counter this approach. Repetitive textures are well-known and present no problems in the carpet-making industry. In renderings, however, they are rarely used for reproducing carpet patterns, even when they inevitably have the same effect. The problem is that, in practice, it is indeed not easy to avoid using repetitive textures. The first option is not to use textures but to use a color instead. The second is to use a procedural texture, which is a pattern calculated during the rendering process using a formula usually involving a random number generator, which means the textures do not repeat themselves and therefore look somewhat like natural materials. A third option is to use a hand-drawn

16

Dominik Lengyel, Catherine Toulouse

Fig. 7

Fig. 8 a–b

Fig. 9 a–c

Fig. 10 a–c

17

The Production Process for the Digital Image in Architecture

Fig. 11 a–b

Fig. 12 a–b

Fig. 13 a–b

Fig. 14 a–b

18

Dominik Lengyel, Catherine Toulouse

texture, virtual or analog, which is usually projected orthogonally onto the virtual model and is the preferred variant in the games industry [Fig. 14b]. Interestingly, the variant generally perceived as particularly realistic, namely hand-drawn textures, is comparable to modeling with very few additional requirements, that is to say free-form modeling without prefabricated elements, such as NURBS modeling.

Finally, it has to be said that using repetitive textures as a makeshift solution must not be confused with their deliberate use as repetitive ornamentation. The latter can now also be seen in built architecture in a way suggestive of a digital image. However, this is more about being deliberately reminiscent of the digital image.

19

The Production Process for the Digital Image in Architecture

Florian Henrich

The Digital Image as a Medium for Representing Architecture in Journals

1   See the contribution from Florian Henrich, Dominik Lengyel, and Catherine Toulouse, pp. 34–137.

2   For more about the effects of digital design tools on the design process, refer to the contribution by Dominik Lengyel and Catherine Toulouse, pp. 10–19.

The conclusions presented here about the digital image in architecture[1] are based not only on a supplementary examination of the image material from the Schinkel competition but also and mainly on comprehensive research in the two German-language architectural journals *ARCH+* and *Bauwelt* as part of the research project "Architecture Transformed." These conclusions will be considered in more detail in the following pages.

To do this, it is first necessary to look into the distinctive features of the type of images up for debate here. They are design representations used to visualize architecture that has not yet been built. All these images can be said to be unlike photographs, in that they do not show anything that already exists. Instead, they show something that physically does not yet exist, that cannot be visited and experienced in three dimensions, nor can it be photographed. It is present only in medium form as a pictorial representation. It does not matter whether the represented designs are ultimately built in the form shown, or as amended, or not built at all; they are all representations that visually anticipate a future built state. They are prospective in nature. The questions facing all the architectural firms represented here are: How can architecture that does not exist be represented? How can a potential built state be visualized? How can images be used to communicate something that perhaps up to this point exists only as a vague intention, an initial idea?

At the same time, this discussion is less about the architecture itself, the represented buildings, and more about the ways and means of their representation. In primary focus here is not the digital image as an operative visual component in the architectural design process, but rather the visual representation of architecture—the digital image not as a design tool but as a presentation medium.[2] As such, it fulfills the purpose of a representative presentation image and therefore a communicative function primarily directed outward beyond the design process. It could be used for presentation, in a competition, for marketing, advertising, or sales.

Finally, it is a special form of pictorial representation of architecture, namely the digital image as a medium for architectural representation in journals. This is above all relevant in two respects. On the one hand, the digital image in printed form, as a printed product, is considered with the transformations it has in part initiated, taking into account the stage of technical development. From what can be seen in the journals, the aspect of the technical reproducibility of the digital image over the 1990s and beyond plays a central role. The normal practice when it came to duplication of digitally generated visualizations was to take analog photographs on slide film of the image displayed on a computer monitor. On the other hand, the digital image is not considered in isolation here, but within the context of contemporary media publication and reception practices, which in turn are subject to the digital transformation. It is not about the technical image as a purely technical or aesthetic phenomenon but about a specific sector of the multifarious architectural image practice, about the actual use of digital architectural images in the media context of the journal.

21

3 See Florian Henrich, "Die Diskussion des digitalen Bildes in den Architekturzeitschriften," in *Rendering / Visualisierung* (Begriffe des digitalen Bildes, 5), ed. Hubert Locher, Dominik Lengyel, Florian Henrich, and Catherine Toulouse, Munich 2024, pp. 28–54. DOI: https://doi.org/10.5282/ubm/epub.109218

For a research project such as the one conducted here, journals offer two advantages that can hardly be overestimated. One is that they provide information through images and text; the second is that they can be evaluated both qualitatively and quantitatively. The two architectural journals forming the focus of the research, *ARCH+* and *Bauwelt*, supply not only a continuous stream of current image material over the period studied that can be collated, analyzed, and interpreted, but also descriptive, reflective, and instructive statements in a wide range of text formats, such as articles, reports, or commentaries that reflect the then-contemporary opinions and experiences. They allow researchers the opportunity to trace the development of the digital image as a medium for representing architecture during the change from the analog to the digital age and at the same time to discursively reconstruct the ongoing debate at the time in its chronology, stages, and main conclusions. It is also possible to quantify the frequency of different image phenomena from the reconstructed history of these published images by simple counting, and set down some empirical foundations. In this way, it is possible to make some generalized statements and assign an exemplary representative character based on specific cases to the observations made in the journals, at least within the framework of this study. The image will be the focus here, while its discussion is explored elsewhere.[3]

It was originally intended to study at least four periodicals in the journal research, adding the Italian magazine *domus* and the Spanish journal *El Croquis* to the German *ARCH+* and *Bauwelt*, but it was soon realized that with the aim of complete sifting this amount of work under the given project brief would prove unmanageable for reasons of practicality. The study was therefore restricted to the two journals *ARCH+* and *Bauwelt*. However, all the issues published in the forty-one years between 1980 and 2020 were leafed through page by page and evaluated, although project requirements meant only the first six months' journals were collected for 2020. A total of 413 images and 263 texts from 190 issues of *ARCH+* as well as 1,740 images and 162 texts from around 1,800 issues of *Bauwelt* were classified and recorded. Altogether they form the corpus of material upon which the study is based.

On this quantitative level alone, it becomes clear how very different the two journals are in their weighting of image and text, and how they would be an almost perfect complement for one another in a study like this precisely because of this difference. Without looking more closely at the tenor of the content and the journalistic practices of the journals over the course of their history, the two journals adopt different stances and roles as publishers of architecture in the Federal Republic of Germany and later in a reunited Germany in accordance with their self-image and programmatic aim. This is relevant to the research in two main respects: while *Bauwelt* informs readers chronologically about the current happenings in architecture, *ARCH+* is an actor with a definite political aim in the current architectural discourse. While *Bauwelt* represents the greater part of architectural development in the present, *ARCH+* takes more of an emphatic avant-garde position in striving to identify and critically reflect on topics relevant to society in their early stages.

22

Florian Henrich

4   Nikolaus Kuhnert, "Zu diesem Heft: Rechnergestütztes Entwerfen," in *ARCH+*, 1984, 77 (Nov.), p. 25.

5   Wolfgang Beck, "Computer im Architekturbüro," in *Bauwelt*, 79, 1988, 45 (25 Nov.), pp. 1921, 1951, here p. 1921.

6   *Bauwelt*, 107, 2016, 33 (26 Aug.): "Ungebautes inszenieren—Architektur verkaufen."

7   "Berichte und Projekte" (*ARCH+*-Zeitung), in *ARCH+*, 1984, 77 (Nov.), pp. 4–9, here p. 5.

8   Felix Zwoch, "Brauchte die Bauwelt ein Re-Design? Muss sie mit dem Zeitgeist Schritt halten?," in *Bauwelt*, 97, 2006, 37 (1 Oct.), p. 2.

9   Boris Schade-Bünsow and Kaye Geipel, "Im neuen Takt," in *Bauwelt*, 107, 2016, 34 (9 Sept.), p. 11.

This is apparent specifically with respect to the examination of the computer and its entrance into architectural practice in Germany toward the middle of the 1980s. Whereas *ARCH+* in its first thematic issue about the computer in 1984 establishes a "concurrence and difference in the content and significance of the developments," which "today go by the names […] Computer Aided Design and postmodernism,"[4] in *Bauwelt*'s first issue about computers four years later, a letter to the editor speaks of "the 'first experiences' still ongoing at the end of 1988, when in fact these experiences had been in 1984."[5] Accordingly, the earliest digital images were not in *Bauwelt*, but in *ARCH+*. However, it is the other way around when it comes to the discussion of the digital image, with *Bauwelt* publishing the only thematic issue about the topic by either of the two journals between 1980 and 2020.[6]

In general, the two journals differ clearly from one another in their image practice as well as in their basic relationship to the image. Whereas *Bauwelt* with its "redesign" in 2006 granted the image a considerably greater standing than before, an obvious reaction to a development that is already established practice in the typical architectural consultancy, the content of *ARCH+* appears to continue a distanced, occasionally skeptical, almost mistrustful relationship with images—as was already being expressed at the start of the 1980s in the criticism of "personal cults" of the postmodern "conveyed via drawings"[7]—without, however, making this critical relationship with the image itself the object of reflection. While the example of *Bauwelt* makes clear that the presence of the digital image among the media in the architectural discourse is caused not only by technical developments but also by editorial decisions, topics such as the pictorial representation of architecture, the necessity of its representation via media, and the subsequent consequences for the perception and reception of architecture are aspects that remain for the most part characteristically ignored in *ARCH+*. Overall, it can be stated that for both journals—putting aside a few exceptions, such as the discussion of technical aspects, above all in the first half of the 1990s—the digital image is hardly explored as a topic. A detailed discussion of its qualities as a medium for architectural representation never takes place.

In line with this different relationship to the image, a far greater number of digital images are found in *Bauwelt*—"the only architecture journal in Germany ever to appear weekly,"[8] until eventually it would be published "in a fortnightly rhythm"[9] from 2016—and particularly in the competition part, where visualizations of not yet built designs are continually and very frequently published. In both cases, the journals are published in German. However, the coverage of the international competition news, as well as the discursive debate of contemporary transnational topics, also allows an eye to be kept on the international dimension of the development of the digital architectural image, at least to some extent. The two journals have other things in common in terms of content: Firstly, the protagonists themselves always get a chance to speak, so that the contemporary view of the participating person on their own practices is expressed. Secondly, there are always current images and thus contemporary compositional modes, fashions, booms, and trends, which can be traced in their aesthetic development.

23

10 Cf. Berliner Volksbank eG (ed.),
    *150 Jahre Schinkel-Wettbewerb.
    Preisgekrönte Ideen und Projekte*,
    exhib. cat., Berlin 2006.

The journal research deliberately compared an image-heavy and a text-heavy medium. It must be borne in mind that the published images in the journals have their own chronology, and this is not guaranteed to agree with that of architectural practice as a whole. The arrival of some technical innovations and image design trends is delayed or never appears in built form. On the other hand, image phenomena may appear to have significant potential, but their effects are not seen everywhere in practice. However—according to the hypothesis—the course of development of the digital image as a medium for representing design, its stages and consequences, may well become transferable on a widespread scale. Therefore, when "the journals" are referred to in general terms in the following, this does not necessarily always mean both *ARCH+* and *Bauwelt*, just as it should be implied that the statements made here could also apply at least to some extent to other areas of architectural image practice. The quantitative statements in particular have a heuristic character, as they do not reflect the absolute frequencies of image phenomena but above all highlight their relationships in volume to one another and their changes over time.

Schinkel competition

An additional source of reference is image material from the Schinkel competition obtained from the inventories of the Architectural Museum of the Technical University of Berlin. This material serves to supplement the perspectives of the representation of architecture in practice by examples of images produced by the students and newly qualified architects, who do not have the same resources and opportunities as large architectural offices or professional external visualization studios. The Schinkel Prize has been awarded by the Association of Architects and Engineers of Berlin-Brandenburg (AIV) in memory of the Prussian architect, city planner, and painter Friedrich Schinkel (1781–1841) since 1852 and is one of the best-known young talent awards for prospective architects in Germany. The Schinkel is an ideas competition divided into various categories, where the ideas are not subject to the pressure of immediate implementation.[10]

Starting point: Architectural representation at the beginning of the 1980s

The aim of the journal research is to look at architectural representation practice over the last four decades, from 1980 to the present, during the age of transition from analog to digital, and to trace the development of the digital image as a medium of architectural representation by considering examples in a media selection from this practice. In the same way as there has been a fundamental change from the analog to the digital age over the last forty years, which still continues and advances, there has also been a fundamental transformation of architectural representation with the change of media from the analog to the digital image. The digital image, sweepingly described for the most part as rendering, has created an image form sui generis that did not exist before. The pictorial

24

Florian Henrich

11 Heinrich Klotz, "Die Revision der Moderne," in *Die Revision der Moderne. Postmoderne Architektur 1960–1980*, ed. Heinrich Klotz, Munich 1984, pp. 7–11, here p. 11.

12 Mathias Schreiber, "Einleitung," in *Architekturzeichnungen HPP 1978–1988*, Munich 1989, pp. 5–7, here p. 5.

13 Florian Zimmermann, "Die Axonometrie," in *Die Architekturzeichnung. Vom barocken Idealplan zur Axonometrie*, ed. Winfried Nerdinger with assist. of Zimmermann, Munich 1986, p. 182.

14 "Sehen was man sieht. Ein Preisausschreiben der Bauwelt," in *Bauwelt*, 66, 1975, 18 (9 May), p. 535.

15 "Gesehen was man sah. Ergebnis des Bauwelt-Preisausschreibens," in *Bauwelt*, 66, 1975, 26 (11 July), p. 731.

16 Ulrich Conrads, "[Editorial]," in *Bauwelt*, 66, 1975, 38/39 (10 Oct.), no pagination.

17 Ekhart Berckenhagen, "Warum präsentiert die Kunstbibliothek Berlin in einer Ausstellung Zeichnungen des Architekten Gerd Neumann?," in *Gerd Neumann: Architekten-Zeichnungen 1960–1978*, exhib. cat., Berlin 1978, no pagination.

18 Gerd Neumann, "Zeichnungen eines Architekten—Architektenzeichnungen?," in *Gerd Neumann*, no pagination (fourth page).

representation of future architecture has become bolder and brighter, more lavish, sometimes more pompous and monumental, but also more illusionistic, suggestive, and persuasive. Above all, however, it has become more perceptible, clearer—in a word, more *vivid*. After a phase of pictorial abstraction and graphic reduction, with the arrival of rendering the image has undergone a re-evaluation.

This is seen particularly clearly in comparison with the situation of architecture representation at the beginning of the 1980s, the starting point of this study. This shows itself on the one hand through its paradigm of abstraction, and on the other through its shift toward seeing drawing as an aesthetically valuable, recognized, and customary vehicle for subjective artistic expression, both embedded in the efforts to evaluate architecture as an autonomous genre of art in reaction to the technical and functional orientation of building practice in the 1960s and '70s.

The efforts to achieve autonomy for architecture as art had begun by the middle of the 1960s, but to some extent this topic was discussed even earlier in various countries under different guises as a critique of the modern. This movement has intensified since the "early seventies"[11] under the term of the postmodern, accompanied on the representational level as the "scene of this rebellion"[12] above all by a "resuscitation of axonometry"[13] but also of the perspective and other drawn forms of architectural representation. In 1975, for instance, *Bauwelt* ran a drawing competition with the cautious aim of "getting some idea of what and how architects draw today"[14] and was surprised by the result. On the one hand, there was a considerable response, while on the other, "the drawings were without exception of a quality no one had anticipated."[15] What's more, according to Ulrich Conrads, the entries showed "just how far away architects still are from being blinkered specialists, despite these miserable times. [...] The rigid suppression of 'artistic thinking' by a partially perverted architectural practice has not been able to entrap hearts, minds, and eyes."[16] Likewise, Ekhart Berckenhagen, as the organizer of the exhibition arising from the competition at the Berlin Kunstbibliothek three years later, is of the opinion that the level of artistic quality is an "astonishing fact, given that people still assume today, usually without reason, that architects do not 'draw,' but create only schematic building designs."[17] This is also reinforced by the exhibited winner of the competition, Gerd Neumann, with reference to the initial question about the current status of drawings in architectural practice:

"This question was, in view of the observed superficial economization of building, the temporary, explicitly programmatic desensualization of planning and the strict 'functionalization' even of drawings—which had been going on for at least three years beforehand—much too well-founded. In the meantime, however, everything has been resolved. At last, architects are drawing again. Criticism, crises, and recollections have prompted the reartification and the discussion about the autonomy of architecture and with that revived the architectural drawing to the standards of the beaux-arts tradition."[18]

These postmodern endeavors bring with them a full-blown drawing boom that finds its way everywhere in German-speaking architectural journalism by the beginning of the 1980s. A characteristic example is the first issue of the architectural journal *Daidalos* in 1981, which is

25

The Digital Image as a Medium for Representing Architecture in Journals

19 Anna Teut, "Einleitung," in *Daidalos*, 1981, 1 (15 Sept.): "Die Zeichnung als Medium der Abstraktion," pp. 12–14, here p. 14.

20 Heinrich Klotz, "Die Architekturzeichnung als Medium einer neuen Ästhetik," in *Jahrbuch für Architektur 1981/1982*, Braunschweig and Wiesbaden 1981, pp. 150–51, here p. 151.

21 Klotz, "Die Revision der Moderne," p. 231.

22 Werner Oechslin, "Editorial," in *Daidalos*, 1987, 25 (15 Sept.): "Die verführerische Zeichnung," p. 23.

23 Wolfgang Meisenheimer, "Die funktionale und die poetische Zeichnung," in *Daidalos*, 1987, 25 (15 Sept.), pp. 111–20, here p. 119.

24 Ibid., p. 120.

25 Werner Durth, "Gebrochene Spiegel: Reflexionen über einen Atelierbesuch bei Helmut Jacoby," in *Daidalos*, 1987, 25 (15 Sept.), pp. 92–105, here p. 93. Cf. also Florian Henrich, "Das Analoge im Digitalen. Entwurfsvisualisierung zwischen Partizipation und Fotorealismus," in *Lens On. Fotografieren in architektonischen Entwurfsprozessen der Moderne*, ed. Tobias Becker, Teresa Fankhänel, Dennis Jelonnek, and Sarine Waltenspül, Berlin 2023, pp. 13–26.

26 Cf. Henrich, "Die Diskussion."

27 Kuhnert, "Zu diesem Heft." "Excitement" refers to postmodernism, "silence" to the computer.

28 Meisenheimer, "Die funktionale", p. 120.

dedicated to "the drawing as a medium of abstraction." The journal states convincingly "that the numerous exhibitions of architectural drawings, the vivid treatment of architectural graphics do not happen by accident. [...] Impoverishment, simplification, and neglect demand correction."[19] Just as Heinrich Klotz writes in the same year in *Jahrbuch für Architektur*: "Not only the technical and factual, but also the commercial violation of the architectural drawing over recent years has resulted in the necessary counteractive tendencies appearing on the paper. Elaborate isometric and perspective drawings [...] create a new interpretation of reality that extends far beyond architecture."[20] In this sense Klotz sees, for instance, in the drawing style of Oswald Mathias Ungers, a "counterargument against the designs for functionalistic buildings of the postwar period, which come close to raw, technical construction drawings. To this can be added the ponderously detailed presentation drawing with all the lifestyle-defining but trivial furnishings of the 50s and 60s was quite suddenly passé."[21]

However, within only a few years, people criticized this boom as the "new drawing cult"[22] because in the meantime, in addition to "the necessity of communication [...] other desires of the draftsmen for representation that were detached from everyday office considerations"[23] stepped into the drawing practice. Thus, according to the second *Daidalos* issue on the subject, which appeared in 1987 under the title "Die verführerische Zeichnung" (The seductive drawing), in "the eighties [...], in addition to the functional and rational sides of representation, some poetic, irrational characteristics were ever more clearly emerging."[24] According to Werner Durth, this tendency toward graphical "mystification of three-dimensionality" fueled the need for clarity in architectural representation, so that there was now "a growing demand for concrete drawings that functioned as mediators between the architectural design and the assessment by clients, financiers, and the critical public."[25]

This was roughly the situation when the computer made its entry on a broad front into architectural practice in Germany around the mid-1980s,[26] as Nikolaus Kuhnert highlights in 1984 in *ARCH+* with his observation of "concurrence and difference" of "Computer Aided Design and postmodernism." He goes on to state "that both developments [...] provoked extremely different reactions: on one side, hysterical excitement; dismayed silence on the other."[27] Not least, this shows a negative causal link between the drawing boom and the onset of digitalization. At the same time, in a 1987 article in *Daidalos*, it is judged "fortunate that the magic of the undefinable and unprogrammable is beginning to assert itself with the increasing capabilities of computers and electronic media."[28] The more visible the computer becomes as a tool in practice, the more the drawing gains in importance as a medium of individual artistic expression in the face of this supposed threat—typical signs of an imminent change of media.

Thilo Hilpert describes this historical coincidence of the re-evaluation of architecture as art and incipient computerization in 1988 under the heading "Paradoxical Simultaneity: Automation and the Art of Drawing" as follows:

"The onset of new technical media first begins to show five or six years earlier at the universities of applied sciences, first of all in mechanical and other engineering departments. This gives rise to

Florian Henrich

29 Thilo Hilpert, *Geometrie der Architekturzeichnung. Einführung in Axonometrie und Perspektive*, Braunschweig and Wiesbaden 1988, p. 125.

30 Cf. e.g. Walter Ehlers, Gernot Feldhusen, and Carl Steckeweh (ed.), *CAD: Architektur automatisch?* (Bauwelt Fundamente, 76), Braunschweig and Wiesbaden 1986.

31 Hilpert, *Geometrie*, p. 124.

32 Cf. in this context Teresa Fankhänel and Andres Lepik (ed.), *The Architecture Machine. The Role of Computers in Architecture*, exhib. cat. Munich, Basel 2020.

33 Werner Oechslin, "'Rendering'—Die Darstellungs- und Ausdrucksfunktion der Architekturzeichnung," in *Daidalos*, 1987, 25 (15 Sept.), pp. 68–77, here p. 71.

34 Werner Oechslin, "Von Piranesi zu Libeskind. Erklären mit Zeichnen," in *Daidalos*, 1981, 1 (15 Sept.), pp. 15–19, here p. 15.

35 Oechslin, "'Rendering,'" p. 68.

36 Winfried Nerdinger, "Vom barocken Planriß zur Axonometrie—Stufen der Architekturzeichnung in Deutschland," in *Die Architekturzeichnung. Vom barocken Idealplan zur Axonometrie*, ed. Winfried Nerdinger, Munich 1986, pp. 8–18, here p. 9.

37 Ibid., p. 10.

38 Ibid., p. 13.

39 Ibid., p. 16. Cf. also Florian Zimmermann, "Die Wettbewerbszeichnung um 1900," in *Die Architekturzeichnung. Vom barocken Idealplan zur Axonometrie*, ed. Winfried Nerdinger with assist. of Zimmermann, Munich 1986, p. 138.

40 See B. Herbert Kiefer, "Renderverbot. Wie man im Saarland die Chancengleichheit bei Wettbewerben erhöhen will," in *Bauwelt*, 101, 2010, 11 (12 Mar.), pp. 12–13.

a paradoxical simultaneity that juxtaposes a renaissance of complicated manual drawing techniques in architectural graphics and an explosion of new graphical creation techniques."[29]

In accord with the tenor of the time concurrently articulated in journals as well as elsewhere,[30] Hilpert considers the contemporary development as an epochal turning point that provides an opportunity to pause and reflect:

"The emerging technical changes arrive at the same time as a revolution in the art of drawing. However, what are the effects on thinking in three dimensions, on architectural thought? [...] The technicalization of drawing and projection can make sense to us only after this question has been clarified."[31]

Historical continuities

These brief sketches of the status quo of architectural representation at the beginning of the 1980s not only define a point of departure whence this study of the digital image in architecture arches across time to the recent past, but also provide the historical framework within which its findings are set. Even today, around thirty years later, this kind of reflective introspection appears to be called for again.[32]

However, as a look further back in the history of architectural representation shows, the digital architectural image is neither a completely new nor a genuine digital phenomenon, but to some extent the current expression of a recurring trend in a larger cyclical context.

This begins with the word *rendering*. According to Werner Oechslin, the term refers to the "highly traditional beaux-arts school" and the "genre of the architectural drawing based on pictorial effects"[33] it cultivated after it had "adopted the representational and illusionistic possibilities of painting"[34] in the eighteenth century. From this time on, the designing architect also "made use of the special skills of a draftsman and an architectural artist."[35] According to Winfried Nerdinger, in the nineteenth century "architectural drawings in Germany increasingly took on the character of paintings," the pictorial "integration of the architectural design into an environment that is no longer schematized, but one treated on an equal footing with almost anecdotal staffage and a completely new colorfulness in the sense of a near-realistic architectural *veduta*."[36] However, in the second half of the nineteenth century, this "new level of reality and illusion of the presentation of architectural design"[37] led to critics increasingly labeling this painterliness "as 'trivial' and flatly rejecting the perspective."[38] This development ended up going so far in Germany that, after the First World War, "an increasing number of design competition rules forbade the use of color and regarded perspectives as unwelcome, believing that anonymity would allow the jury to make a more impartial assessment."[39]

The history of the architectural representation shows remarkable parallels to the development and discussion of the digital architectural image as we have discussed here. Even today, since the beginning of the 2010s, there have again been quite a few examples of architectural competitions in which renderings have been expressly prohibited.[40] On the one hand, this gives rise to the impression of advancing innovation

27

41 Chris Dähne, "Die 'analogen Bilder' digitaler Architektur," in *Wolkenkuckucksheim*, 25, 2021, 40, pp. 113–24.

42 Cf. Hubert Locher, "'Andere Zeiten, andere Bilder!' Historienmalerei und Fotografie," in *Vorbilder / Nachbilder. Die fotografische Lehrsammlung der Universität der Künste Berlin 1859–1930*, ed. Ulrich Pohlmann, Dieter Schenk, and Anastasia Dittmann, exhib. cat. Munich and Berlin, Cologne 2020, pp. 226–43.

43 Manfred Sack, "Zeichnende Architekten und ein Architekt, welcher Zeichner ist," in Peter Wels, *Architekturzeichnungen*, with a foreword from Sack, Hamburg 1993, pp. 7–20, here p. 9.

of the technical media; while on the other, the type and methods of the compositional means, the aims and purposes of their use, as well as the accompanying discursive and normative patterns demonstrate significant continuities.

As Chris Dähne has pointed out, however, the historical connection assumed by Nerdinger between the manner in which architecture is represented and the prevailing comprehension of architecture no longer seems to apply to the digital architectural image. They have become much more dissociated from one another as a result of digitalization.[41] Just as the computer can, in principle, be used to create and implement any conceivable form, it can also be used in principle to imitate any graphical process and any historical style of art. An answer to the question of how the genuine digital style that adequately reflects the technical conditions of the present would look is much more likely to be found with those who use the digital visualization tools than with the tools themselves. The prevailing ideal for today is still the continuous paradigm of digital photorealism, which is based on and strives for the photograph's promise of reality, the representation of a design to look like a photograph, as if the presently projected future building were already a photographed reality. It is an equivocal and in no way completely defined idea that refers to a pictorial approach that reaches back beyond the painting of the 1970s to the art of the nineteenth century.[42]

Digital architectural image practice

As emphasized time and time again in contemporary commentaries, the return to abstract axonometry as an adequate form of representation for a re-evaluation of architecture as art was fed above all by the criticism of the vividness of the perspective. As Manfred Sack pointedly summarizes in 1993, the key point of this criticism was that "the perspective drawing is seen principally as a deceptive maneuver, designed to mislead not only clients ('laypeople') but also jurors well versed in the field ('experts'), and confuse them by representing the planned building as more dramatic and magnificent or innocuous than it is in reality."[43] Today's digital architectural image practice appears to be the direct opposite of the view at the beginning of the 1980s.

The digital image propagated a new desire for the image in the pictorial representation of architecture. As rendering achieved success on a massive scale as the new, popular standard in the first half of the 2000s, the pictorial drawing again performed its triumphant march in architectural representation—moving away from the abstract representation, understood only by those in the know, and toward an easy-to-understand, graphic perspective. The representative figure experiences a new boom, the architectural design becomes an object of graphic scenery. The process of design becomes graphic and so does the visual representation of the designed object. This new vividness appears as a significant feature of the digital image in architecture. The representation of architecture once more becomes realistic, perspective, illusionistic; it becomes colorful; it becomes atmospheric, suggestive, emotional, in part sentimental and emotive—and, above all, photorealistic.

28

Florian Henrich

44 Ulrich Conrads, "Sieben Psychogramme," in *Daidalos*, 1987, 25 (15 Sept.), pp. 37–41, here pp. 37–38.

45 Marian Behaneck, "Rechner-gestützte Darstellungsverfahren," in Marian Behaneck, Dieter J. Heimlich, and Peter Wossnig, *Vom CAAD zum Bild. Architektur als fotorealistische Erlebniswelt*, Neustadt a. d. W. 1991, pp. 43–130, here p. 129.

46 Ibid., p. 125.

47 See the contribution from Hubert Locher, pp. 138–149.

48 Oechslin, "'Rendering,'" p. 68.

49 Cf. e.g. the advertising supplement in *Deutsche Bauzeitung*, 47, 1913, 90 (8 Nov.).

In this regard, what Ulrich Conrads stated in 1987 in his look back on the practice of representation from a historical point of view up to the 1970s applies to the same extent to the digital architectural image:

"The architect, if he sees himself as an autonomous artist or as a master builder concerned with providing services, must carry his ideas to the market. He must also make his ideas understandable [...] so that he finds clients and employers who are [...] able to identify with the building concept and the architecture. [...] Colleagues are always involved and pay suspicious attention to any generally comprehensible graphical creation that [...] counterfeits reality and anticipates it even before a single stone has been placed. And already, viewed from this side of the competition, a broad consensus about the type and means of architectural representation is establishing itself. It brings to light what we have become accustomed to calling the zeitgeist."[44]

Here Conrads is addressing the development of stylistic tendencies and fashionable trends of image design from the specific contexts, in which the architectural image is used as a representative display image, in particular for the purposes of presentation, advertisement, or sales. This applies likewise to the digital architectural images used in competitions, on the architect's website, in journals, as well as in real estate brochures or on the site publicity board. Even today, a discrepancy exists between practice and discourse: while rendering is used practically everywhere, it is, at the same time, subject to the massive criticism that has been observed since the 2010s in the journals. The narrative arc when looking at architectural representation over the past forty years describes how the digital image, after its establishment in architectural practice from the mid-1990s, gradually loses the "appeal of the new, the spectacular,"[45] after which the "image-promoting effect"[46] of rendering ultimately results in dissatisfaction and a search for alternative digital approaches to image design. After the hype of the early years, the digital image to some extent develops an image problem, which manifests itself in "rendering bans."

Rendering has an ambivalent status for various reasons. One may be its use both in architecture and in real estate, where it serves decidedly strategic marketing and advertising purposes. Here the suggestiveness of the digital image increases its effectiveness as an advertising sales tool, which it was specifically formulated to be during the 1990s.[47] One of the roots of the skepticism toward rendering, which can be heard even within the architecture community itself, at least on the discursive level, may lie in this dual role of communicating the design and selling the product. This skepticism is further increased by many architects not creating their own renderings but outsourcing the job to external visualization studios. It is a perfectly ordinary and widespread practice, which can be confirmed with a simple internet search. This service reinforces the character of the image as a product and gives critics the opportunity to differentiate. However, as Oechslin has already explained, this type of "division of labor"[48] goes back to the eighteenth century. The advertising sections of journals have contained offers from companies providing external design visualization services since before the First World War.[49] The digital architectural image oscillates between artistic ambition on the one hand and functional purpose on the other, in

29

50 Neumann, "Zeichnungen eines Architekten," no pagination (fourth page).

51 Hilpert, *Geometrie*, p. 137.

the same way as architecture is itself a hybrid of art and technology. Neither excludes the other, nor can the pair be separated.

The ambivalence may also stem from the fact that digital design visualizations involve ephemeral images intended only for temporary use. They serve to illustrate a building for as long as it does not yet physically exist, at which time it could simply be photographed. This can be seen on the websites of architectural consultancies: as soon as the design has been built, the photorealistic anticipation of what it would look like disappears from the website and is replaced by actual photographs of the real building. To a certain extent, the rendering bridges the visual void between the design competition and the completed building, and represents an interim solution that is obviously not seen as the equivalent of, or a full substitute for, a true photograph of the actual architecture.

A further point of criticism, which is also heard in the journals, relates to the sheer quantity of digital images, their vast worldwide distribution, for example via media channels such as Instagram, as well as the concurrently developing "consensus about the type and means of architectural representation," as Conrads called it in 1987, specifically the tendency toward standardization of representation in the sense of a fashionable phenomenon that is perceived as inflationary from a certain point in its quantitative expansion.

However, what is responsible for igniting criticism time and time again is above all the suggestive photorealism of the digital image, that is to say the visual impact of those visualizations that generally are described as renderings. They try not only to depict their subject, the future building, as realistically as possible, as if it were already built reality, but also to have it appear in the most advantageous light, both literally and figuratively. As Manfred Sack already remarked in his criticism of the perspective drawing, photorealistic renderings are also criticized for concealing or distorting the actual architectural qualities of the design by creating an illusionistic staging that appears to be photographic reality, thus eluding critical assessment. The supposedly simulative nature of the representation prevents not only any kind of fantasy on the part of the observer but also any need to exercise imagination, or likewise any possibility of projecting themselves into the image, which results in the photorealistic architectural image being consumed like a commodity. Digital photorealism leads people to confuse the object represented with its representation and, according to Gerd Neumann, get entangled "only too easily in judging [...] architecture by the appeal and skill of its representation"[50] instead of against specific architectural standards and criteria. The staging—the surrounding scene set up using compositional elements—to some extent pushes itself in front of the depicted design or overlays it, and thus distracts from the actual subject of the representation.

As already mentioned, this point of criticism is neither new nor applicable only to the digital architectural image. It is much more about a traditional conflict of architectural representation that exists in the polarity of the image and the drawing, of vividness and abstraction, of fiction and information. According to Hilpert, this "ambivalence of the autonomous, painterly image of reality or the drawing as a model for the architectural construction,"[51] which also characterizes the digital image,

30

Florian Henrich

52 Cf. Hubert Locher and Rolf Sachsse (ed.), *Architektur Fotografie. Darstellung—Verwendung—Gestaltung*, Berlin and Munich 2016.

ultimately refers to the fundamental relationship of architecture and image. On the one hand, the critics repeatedly refer to the shortcomings of the image—of the drawing, of the rendering—as a basis for the assessment of the design and to the deceptiveness, fragmentation, and subjectivity of the representation, which distorts objective understanding and evaluation. On the other, in practice the design is increasingly staged pictorially in a scene, and something is added that goes beyond the purely architectural. In fact, however, the visual reproduction of built or designed architecture is always accompanied by compromises, losses, and distortions. These visual transformations affect not only the experiential quality of the building as a spatial, three-dimensional object capable of being experienced only through motion, but also its practical utility value as residential or commercial premises. Nevertheless, architecture relies on media communication through images, not only as the design, the imagined future state, but also as a realized but immobile object that otherwise would be viewable only by physically visiting it. Every pictorial representation of architecture—the photorealistic rendering just as much as the drawn perspective and the photographic image—remains an interpretation, a graphical staging, like it or not, irrespective of how functionally or suggestively it has been designed.[52]

The absence, at least from the journals, of any discussion of the digital image or even the subject of architectural representation in general, the self-evident nature of the ubiquitous digital image practice on the one hand, and the criticism leveled at it on the other are possibly three decisive factors influencing why a comprehensive examination of the digital image, and above all of the digital presentation image, as a medium of architectural representation has so far taken place only to a limited extent. Accordingly, the differentiated use of its compositional material and the relatively frequent associated artistic viewpoint of art history are hardly ever taken into consideration.

The digital architectural image in journals

The story emerging from the journal research into over forty years of the practice of architectural representation, from 1980 to 2020, covers the period from the re-evaluation of the architectural drawing as an artistic medium and the awakening need for vivid architectural representation in the age of the postmodern, over the entrance of the digital image into architectural practice and the new digital image boom, and on to the surfeit of digital images and the search for alternatives from the mid-2010s. In certain respects, this development finds expression in *Bauwelt* in the quantitative graph of the digital architectural image [(Fig. 1)]. It can be clearly seen that the digital image first appears in significant numbers in the middle of the 1990s. However, it takes only ten years before it climbs to its first high peak on the graph. While its emergence in the journals keeps everyone waiting, its wider propagation builds up speed.

Qualitatively, a significant change in the aesthetic appearance of the digital architectural image and the compositional methods employed is observed as arising from both the progress of digital visualization techniques and the artistic development of the image. At the start of the 2000s, digital architectural representation achieved such levels

31

The Digital Image as a Medium for Representing Architecture in Journals

of practicability and quality that it took over from analog model photography in the journals, which until then had been the dominant image medium for depicting architectural designs. From the second half of the 2000s, there is a more pronounced compositional variance and stylistic differentiation. A curtailed account of the last twenty years would describe a significant reversal of the dominant image medium, which changes from a gleaming white or milky, daylight-flooded, transparent, soft-focus mode of representation, by way of a subdued, refined realism with reserved, muted, earthy tones, to a delicate pastel or glaring, thickly applied, golden warm shimmering-light mood, which can escalate into the monumental pathos of a dramatic romance of light, fed from the overpowering force of nature. Between 2000 and 2020, the dominant image mode changes from an airy, light style into something heavier and highly saturated, the complete opposite. There is evidence of a parallel development since the mid-2010s that shows a conscious rejection of conventional digital design visualization and a turn toward alternative approaches to digital image composition based on graphical methods from the analog age [(Fig. 2)].

In fact, the story of the digital image, how it manifested itself in the two journals studied, is considerably more complex and diverse in form than could be exhaustively described in such a broad overview. Considered as a whole, however, it can be said that the digital architectural image contributes little innovation despite its overall stylistic diversity. On the one hand, the photorealistic paradigm dominates from the beginning: the pictorial anticipation of the future building in the mode of the photograph, and with that the suppression of the provisional nature of the design. On the other hand, the central aspect of "atmosphere" relates to the suggestive effect of the image and is also ever present from the beginning. The concept of atmosphere in particular is revealing for the postulate of photorealism as a supposedly deceptively genuine reproduction of reality, because the photorealistic image is not simply intended to depict the future built reality but rather to endow it with an aesthetic added value, which, with the help of the pictorial means described later, elevates it beyond the purely architectural.

The journal research stopped in the second half of 2020, and since then the development of the digital architectural image in terms of a process affected by many factors has of course continued. In addition to the intended pictorial message, the architectural office's attitude to design, and the individual resources for compositional expression, these factors include the technical progress of digital visualization methods as well as the change of stylistic tendencies and fashion trends of image composition. As a fleeting look across the websites of various architectural consultancies might suggest, there seems to be a current trend in image composition toward elegant restraint and refinement of pictorial representation, thus continuing the development of the digital image as a medium of architectural representation as outlined here; whether this is a sign of the rejection of current trends or a further diversification of the present spectrum cannot be said for certain at this point. Despite all trends toward standardization and the volume of criticism, the digital architectural image certainly offers means of expression for an individual and sometimes a high-quality, artistically ambitious, and characteristic composition style.

32

Florian Henrich

Fig. 1: The increasing appearance
of the digital image in *Bauwelt*
(idealized representation)

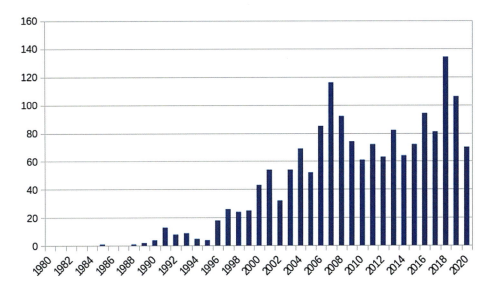

Fig. 2: The gleaming white mode
(red), the golden, warm light mood
(blue), alternative digital compositional approaches (yellow)

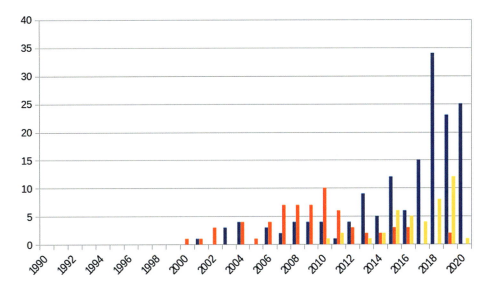

33

The Digital Image as a Medium for Representing Architecture in Journals

Florian Henrich,
Dominik Lengyel,
Catherine Toulouse

The Evolution
of the Digital Image:
The Digital Image in
Architecture 1980–2020

The following compilation consists of fifty-one images showing design visualizations, architectural projects that, at the time of their depiction, did not yet exist in the built state but only as fleeting sketches on paper, as physical models made of materials such as paperboard, wood, or foam, or as virtual 3D models in the computer. They stem from the period between 1980 and 2020 and are either taken from the two German-language architectural journals *ARCH+* and *Bauwelt* or belong to the inventory of the Schinkel competition at the Architectural Museum of the Technical University of Berlin. The quoted project information and descriptions come from the journals.

Initially, it was planned to refer exclusively to original image files held by the architectural practices. However, it turned out that many of the files for these older representations were no longer available or could not be opened with more modern software. It was therefore decided, in cases where the offices contacted could not provide the files, to replace the missing images with photographic reproductions of the illustrations in the journals. This is the reason why the raster pattern of the journal print is visible in some examples.

The fifty-one images from forty years of architectural representation practice are a subjective selection, and yet as representative as possible to reflect a specific development of the digital architectural image like that considered from the point of view of the history of art and the practice of architecture in the research project "Architecture Transformed—Architectural Processes in the Digital Image Space." The project identified various image phenomena, studied their compositional means, and investigated their effects. The findings are linked by the presented selection and the accompanying texts to an exemplary development of the digital image as a medium for architectural representation.

The research is an attempt to draw some general conclusions from the evidence in individual cases within a specific section of the media used in architectural image practice that can be transferred and applied to other areas of architectural representation between 1980 and 2020. The focus is less on the buildings represented than on the types and methods of their representation in images inserted into the ongoing discourse on architecture as visual media through specialist journals. The images are received by the public either flicking through or attentively acquiring knowledge by studying them. Also included are images such as those submitted for the Schinkel competition, which can directly influence career success.

Last but not least, the development of the architectural image, as portrayed here as the change from the analog to the digital age, points to some constant lines, with the result that the development can be spoken of as more of an evolution than a revolution.

35

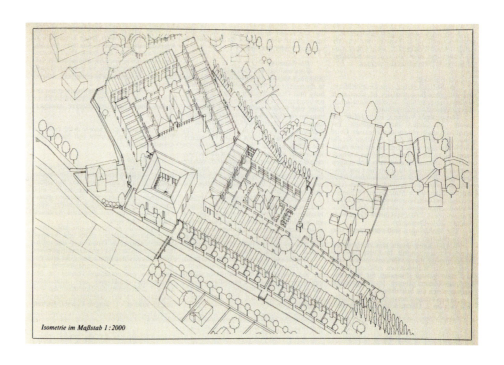

Isometrie im Maßstab 1:2000

1

Jürgen E. Leitner

Residential Development—Schliesselberger Site in Salzburg

Hand drawing
Reproduction of
journal image
in: *Bauwelt*, 71, 1980,
22 (6 June), p. 911

1 The only two exceptions are:
   Barbara Tietze, "Ergonomie
   in Büro und Verwaltung," in
   Bauwelt, 72, 1981, 31 (14 Aug.),
   pp. 1322–25; and Gerd Hamcher,
   "Architekturbüros in der
   Rezession," in *ARCH+*, 1983,
   67 (Mar.), pp. 41–42.

2 Baumgarten, Gerken, Hämmer-
   ling, Riepl, *Datenverarbeitung für
   Architekten*, Stuttgart et al. 1982,
   p. 195.

3 As is also the case here, an axonometric projection is frequently
   and incorrectly described as
   isometric, which is in fact a
   special type of axonometry.

4 Jürgen Leitner, "Das Erbe
   als Vorbild," in *Bauwelt*, 71,
   1980, 22 (6 June), pp. 910–12,
   here p. 910. The design is taken
   from the author's diploma project
   at RWTH Aachen.

5 Ibid., p. 911.

Quite a number of pages must be leafed through in either of the architectural journals from the start of 1980 before the first digital image appears. *ARCH+* and *Bauwelt* contain almost no references to computers at this time. There is not one digital image or computer-generated drawing to be found. The computer is not discussed nor in any other way treated as a separate topic.[1] In architectural practice, as manifested in journals at the beginning of the 1980s, the digital image is not yet in use. This applies not only to the field of visualization but also to the computer in general. From the results of a survey by the Federal Chamber of German Architects dating back to December 1980, "it could be assumed that electronic data processing finds daily use in some form or another in a good 2 percent of all architectural design offices."[2]

As a cursory overview of the 1980 volume of *Bauwelt* shows, architectural designs are generally represented using either photographs of models or graphics produced by hand. Axonometric drawings sit in first place. Less frequently used are elevations and sections, and even more seldom seen are perspectives. Illustrative diagrams or presentation drawings are the exception, likewise sketches, photomontages, and photographs taken with an endoscope. The axonometric drawing, which is produced using an angled parallel projection from a plan or elevation, and the model photograph are by far the most common pictorial forms used for visualizing designs in architectural representational practice as reflected in *Bauwelt* at the start of the 1980s.

The illustration opposite shows one of around thirty axonometric projections found in the forty-eight issues during that first year.[3] The line drawing produced by hand with an ink pen (Rapidograph) is a representative example of the status quo in architectural representation at the beginning of the observation period. Most of these drawings appear extremely reduced, functional, technical, and austere. At the same time, they are instructive and have a specific pictorial quality.

As is the case here: the purism of the lineation, the reduction to elementary basic shapes, and the omission of any kind of graphical forms create an image effect of extreme severity and austerity. At the same time, the ensemble gives an impression of self-containment, with a clear context in which individual architectural components are easily distinguished from one another. This type of representation of a residential project in an urban environment in Salzburg accords with the main design idea to "take the city's characteristic form of development and assimilate it into new urban concepts."[4] Because for "a 'new building,' the historical types can provide models more capable of development than the buildings of 'trivial' functionalism with the plan layouts and building forms of the time."[5] It makes sense, therefore, to show these new buildings in absolute clarity.

37

AXONOMETRIE

Image 2

2

Oswald Mathias Ungers

Competition—
Solar Houses
Melkerei Landstuhl,
Linked Detached Housing

Hand drawing
Reproduction of
journal image
in: *ARCH+*, 1981,
57/58 (July), p. 14

1 Gerd Neumann, "Zeichnungen eines Architekten—Architektenzeichnungen?," in *Gerd Neumann: Architekten-Zeichnungen 1960–1978*, exhib. cat., Berlin 1978, no pagination (fourth page).

2 Heinrich Klotz, "Die Revision der Moderne," in *Die Revision der Moderne. Postmoderne Architektur 1960–1980*, ed. Klotz, Munich 1984, pp. 7–11, here p. 9.

3 Neumann, "Zeichnungen eines Architekten."

4 Vittorio Magnago Lampugnani, *Architektur unseres Jahrhunderts in Zeichnungen. Utopie und Realität*, Stuttgart 1982, p. 16.

5 Florian Zimmermann, "Die Axonometrie," in *Die Architekturzeichnung. Vom barocken Idealplan zur Axonometrie*, ed. Winfried Nerdinger, Munich 1986, pp. 182–83, here p. 182.

6 Heinrich Klotz, *Moderne und Postmoderne. Architektur der Gegenwart 1960–1980*, Braunschweig and Wiesbaden 1984, p. 231.

7 Cf. *Bauwelt*, 71, 1980, 29 (1 Aug.), pp. 1252–54.

8 Lore Ditzen in conversation with Oswald M. Ungers, in *ARCH+*, 1981, 57/58 (July), pp. 12–16, here p. 14.

It is no accident that axonometric projections appear increasingly in architectural journals at the start of the 1980s. Their emergence is directly related to the ongoing attempts since the 1970s to revalue architecture as art, which, as a countermovement to the "observed superficial economic optimization of building, the temporary, almost programmatic desensualization of planning and the strict 'functionalization' of the drawing,"[1] are intent on achieving an architectural design "that no longer proclaims the abstraction of pure stereometric forms but uses the diverse forms of the represented communication of contents and messages."[2] Together with these efforts around this "reartification"[3] of architecture, which is, for the most part, generally described as postmodern, "a crucial re-evaluation of architectural drawing as a specific discipline"[4] is taking place and receiving increased attention at the start of the 1980s, including in German architectural journalism.

At the heart of this drawing boom stands the "revitalization of the axonometric projection."[5] In contrast to perspectives, an axonometric projection does not represent the building in accordance with the rules of human vision, with an illusionistic three-dimensional vanishing point construction, but constructs it as a draftsman would, using the same logic as parallel projection, in other words as a construct that can be understood in its entirety at a glance while at the same time allowing direct visual appreciation of dimensions. Through this characteristic position between image and plan, between vividness and abstraction, fiction and information, the axonometric projection proves to be a genuine architectural process of representation, and therefore the tried-and-tested means for an artistic "revision of the modern."

Architect Oswald Mathias Ungers (1926–2007), whose drawings "set a precedent throughout the world and have become the most widely used style of representation of architecture,"[6] is one of its foremost promoters. The axonometric perspective shown here is captivating because of not just the extraordinary precision of the hand drawing but also the high degree of vividness this drawing achieves. The drawing is based on the layout plan tilted at 45 degrees, from which the verticals extend as parallel lines to the required height. The angle of the image diagonals and the rectangular image format are clearly interpreted—a symmetrical, self-contained construction in mathematical harmony. Like the design itself,[7] its image develops from the elements of the given situation. From the painstaking reproduction of every single brick and plant arises a parametric representation of such opulent figurativeness that it fulfills the purpose of a representative presentation image. Image and plan are synthesized without the inclusion of any elements foreign to the design, to create "an artistic statement with which we can represent our new formal intentions," says Ungers.[8]

39

The Evolution of the Digital Image

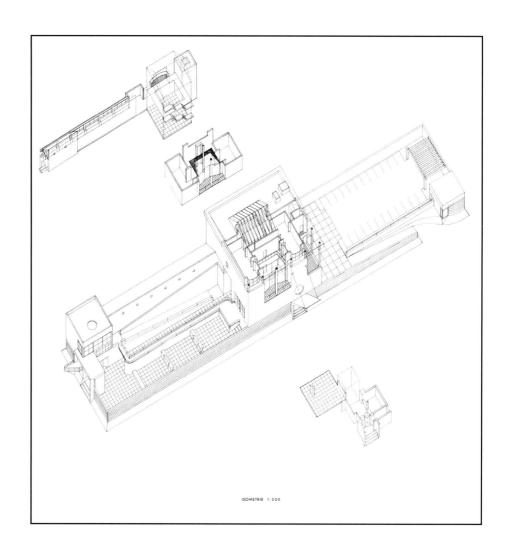

ISOMETRIE 1:200

Image 3

3

David Chipperfield,
Roger Huntley

Schinkel Competition 1981

Hand drawing
Print of the digital copy
Architectural Museum
of the TU Berlin,
Inv. No. SW-A 1981,
01–02

1   Helmut Jacoby, *Neue Architek-
    turdarstellung*, Stuttgart 1981,
    p. 6.

2   Cf. text → Image 17.

Axonometric projections that fulfill the task of an explanatory presentation image can also be found in the image material of the Schinkel competition. The drawing by Ungers provides a fine example of the pictorial quality of axonometry. Its special capability and the high degree of abstraction as a specific form of architectural representation are apparent in this drawing by Chipperfield and Huntley. It shows a plan axonometric projection executed as an exploded view drawing. The building is, so to speak, dismantled into its individual parts of the drawing to make the complex three-dimensional structures hidden in its interior more visible. Several partial views are placed openly visible on other areas of the sheet alongside the overall view. It obliges the observer to relate the individual segments and reassemble them in their head into a whole—a somewhat challenging task that assumes certain cognitive abilities and above all a highly developed ability to imagine things in three dimensions. The axonometric representation has also to be actually read and understood and not simply viewed. It therefore facilitates a specific architectural understanding and distinguishes itself from the purely pictorial consideration of a perspective representation.

At the same time, the drawing embodies the then-contemporary graphical style, as architectural draftsman Helmut Jacoby describes it in the same year:

"Due to its exactness and clarity, black, waterproof ink is still especially suitable for representing modern architecture and remains the draftsman's most treasured medium. [...] It has enjoyed a special popularity as a means of representation due to its extreme precision and excellent economy; indicating neither shadows nor surfaces, its sole means of representation is usually boundary lines mostly drawn in the same thickness."[1]

This description also applies to the drawing by Chipperfield and Huntley. It is equally applicable to the graphical appearance of the early architectural drawings created with the computer that emerged from the mid-1980s as the first digital images in journals. At the beginning of the 1980s, practical architecture representation mainly takes the form of an extremely reduced, decidedly technical drawing style, which—at least to the untrained eye—is hard to distinguish from the first digital architectural representations: hand drawings and computer drawings look similar enough to be confused.

Last but not least, the competition entry from Chipperfield and Huntley makes clear that there is little difference between the quality of representation from students and professionals. As can be seen here, the differences in the representations caused by the available technical equipment are not as severe as those occurring later in the age of digital rendering. At this time, the quality of the representation still depends more on individual artistic capabilities and less on the financial resources of an office.[2]

The Evolution of the Digital Image

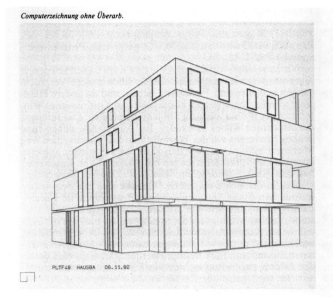

PLTF48 HAUSBA 08.11.82

Image 4

Rüdiger Kramm

Glässingstrasse Darmstadt

CAD drawing and
manual revision
Reproduction of
journal image
in: *ARCH+*, 1984,
77 (Nov.), pp. 40/41

1   Nikolaus Kuhnert, "Zu
    diesem Heft: Rechnergestütztes
    Entwerfen," in *ARCH+*, 1984,
    77 (Nov.), p. 25. Kuhnert has been
    editor of the journal since 1975
    and co-publisher since 1983.
    See *ARCH+*, 2019, 237 (Nov.),
    p. 160.

2   Rüdiger Kramm, "Erfahrungen
    aus dem Alltag," in *ARCH+*, 1984,
    77 (Nov.), pp. 40–43, here p. 41.

3   Ibid.

4   Gerd Neumann, "CAD—Ein Blick
    von draußen," in *ARCH+*, 1984,
    77 (Nov.), p. 65.

The problem of distinguishing between hand and computer drawings becomes still more complicated by the fact that plotted CAD drawings—line drawings created as vector graphics using software from the field of computer-aided design and then transferred to paper by pen plotters—are often revised by hand. This double image from *ARCH+* 77/1984 with the title "Thema: Computer-Aided-Design—Zum Stand der Kunst" provides an instructive example. This thematic issue of *ARCH+* is the first to focus on computers in architecture and discusses the digitalization of design and the consequences for architectural practice. As Nikolaus Kuhnert makes clear in the editorial, this type of "rationalization does not originate on the production side [...], but rather it penetrates the building industry from outside and captures ... the design and planning process itself."[1] However, the initial focus of the debate is less about design itself but above all about the automation of drawing, specifically the preparation of drawings and plans no longer by hand, painstakingly with pen and ink, T-square, and razor blade, but with the computer.

Rüdiger Kramm reports on the advantages and disadvantages in practice of using the new digital drawing tools in his article "Erfahrungen aus dem Alltag," from which the image is taken. According to Kramm, after entering the planned layout into the CAD program, users can

"immediately create elevations and sections, without having to calculate all the dimensions, and last but not least generate perspectives of all kinds from any selected point. Naturally, this appears very attractive. However, on closer inspection and while working with the system, weaknesses also became clear. Comparing a computer drawing with a hand drawing, it is apparent that the graphical representation leaves something to be desired. Furnishings from the computer look downright silly. An axes system could not be created, pillars had to be entered as walls, [...] surface areas, views, elevations, and perspectives were only partially reproduced. [...] Computer-drawn views were therefore not created right from the beginning, because of the anticipated low rate of success, and the drawing quality was not up to the standards of our office."[2]

This experience caused Kramm to come to a rather sobering judgment about the practical possibilities of digital visualization:

"On more detailed inspection, the initially amazing representation of perspectives on the monitor and later on the plotter showed itself to be very poor and was finally used only as a draft. The amount of work involved in entering all the details is considerable and disproportionate to the benefit gained."[3]

The advent of the digital image "in the shadow of the spectacle of the reartification of architecture"[4] is taking place rather slowly in the journals and almost imperceptibly in the mode of the drawing, which, on the one hand, differs in style only slightly from those produced in the current drawing boom and, on the other hand, appears in a hybrid form manually revised in response to the shortcomings of the technology.

43

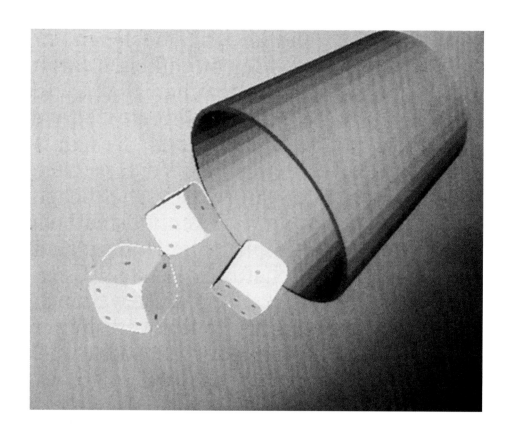

Image 5

5

Reinhard Bögge

3D-Solid Modeling

Rendering
Reproduction of
journal image
in: *Bauwelt*, 76, 1985,
29 (2 Aug.), p. 1163

1   Bernhard E. Bürdek, "Computer
    Aided Design," in *Bauwelt*, 76,
    1985, 29 (2 Aug.), pp. 1162–63,
    here p. 1162.

2   Marian Behaneck, "Rechner-
    gestützte Darstellungsverfahren,"
    in Marian Behaneck, Dieter J.
    Heimlich, and Peter Wossnig,
    *Vom CAAD zum Bild. Architektur
    als fotorealistische Erlebniswelt*,
    Neustadt a. d. W. 1991,
    pp. 43–130, here p. 70.

3   Ibid., p. 75.

4   B. Maier, "2D- oder 3D-CAD?," in
    *CAD-Leitfaden für Architekten.
    Rechnergestütztes Zeichnen und
    Entwerfen*, ed. Michael Pawelski
    and Joachim Winke, Karlsruhe
    1985, pp. 30–32, here p. 32.

As Nikolaus Kuhnert stated in *ARCH+* 77/1984, the digitalization of architectural design and visualization is much less a development that started out in architecture and more one that "penetrates the building industry from outside." The computer is not approaching architectural practice from the artistic side, but rather as a technical innovation above all from the field of mechanical engineering, which the German architectural professions have also seen themselves increasingly confronted by since the mid-1980s. A sign of this is that the first rendering, the first truly digital image as distinct from a digital drawing, that was published in the two journals was not a piece of architecture but a dice cup.

Accordingly, the context of the image is *Bauwelt* vol. 29/1985 on the topic of "Design in Deutschland." It illustrates an article by Bernhard E. Bürdek about computer-aided design arising from a postgraduate course for students of product design at the University of Art and Design Offenbach am Main (HFG) to "prepare students for the changes in work practices resulting from increasing computerization" with the help of "solutions such as those available in the fields of construction, mechanical engineering and architecture etc."[1] It is the first such article on CAD published in *Bauwelt*.

The rendering shows an example of solid modeling, a three-dimensional geometric model created with a CAD program of an object, in this case a dice cup, existing virtually in the computer and available to view on the monitor. As distinct from 3D wire frame modeling, it offers the possibility for rendering digital images. As will be explained later, rendering means "covering the polylines of an object with surfaces using an illumination model,"[2] which not only consists of "deleting the non-visible lines or surfaces of three-dimensional scenery, but also the simulation of lighting effects and material characteristics."[3] That is also what already happens here. The object is a digitally shaded, three-dimensional representation created from a 3D model. The polylines of the cup model can be clearly seen, probably because the available computer capacity would not allow enough polygons to achieve an apparently stepless representation. Calculating the shading, which is mainly responsible for the impression of three-dimensionality, was probably done using the Gouraud method, an illumination model that uses the angle of the surface relative to the light source to calculate its brightness, which allows the cup to look as if it is illuminated from the inside.

Despite these limitations, from the very start, images like these carry the nimbus of photorealism and cast their spell over public and professional viewers in equal measure. So much so that the 1985 publication *CAD-Leitfaden für Architekten* says computers allowed users "to create shading and reflections in representations that come close to achieving the quality standard of photographs of the same object," and that solid modeling in particular produces "a three-dimensional, vivid simulation of the soon-to-be-manufactured reality."[4]

45

Image 6

6

Lucien Kroll

*Les Rocages
Saint-Germain-sur-Vienne*

Rendering
Reproduction of
journal image
in: *ARCH+*, 1985,
83 (Dec.), p. 28

1   Lucien Kroll in conversation
with Kay Friedrichs and
Hans-Jürgen Serwe, "CAD:
Kompliziertheit oder Komplexi-
tät?," in *ARCH+*, 1985, 82 (Dec.),
pp. 25–31, here p. 25.

2   Ibid.

3   Ibid., p. 29.

4   Lucien Kroll, "EDV und
Architektur," in *ARCH+*, 1984,
77 (Nov.), pp. 48–54, here p. 54.

5   Lucien Kroll in conversation,
pp. 25–27.

6   "Atelier Lucien Kroll. Intelligence
artificielle et architecture
naturaliste," in *L'Architecture
d'Aujourd'hui*, 1986, 244 (April),
p. 59. The image is printed on
p. 62.

Quite different from the rendering of the dice cup in the design issue of *Bauwelt*, the first digital image in *ARCH+* that is more than a plotted line drawing comes from current architectural practice. It was created in the studio of the Belgian architect Lucien Kroll (1927–2022) and published in the second issue of *ARCH+* on the subject of computers, which appeared at the end of 1985 under the title "Raum, Zeit und CAD-Architektur."

Kroll, who is particularly well-known for his participative approach and involves the future residents to the greatest extent possible in the planning and design of their housing, is considered "one of the first architects to have fully engaged with the new technology in practice and be open to new possibilities, while criticizing their inherent dangers."[1] The image was created with an in-house CAD program, developed on the one hand "to prevent the industry yet again determining what was possible and what was not," and on the other hand to ensure that "the architecture and not the autonomy of the equipment used should be the primary consideration."[2] The program is called Paysage (French for landscape) and is intended to "allow the designer to work from the landscape to the object rather than only from the object to the landscape."[3] Instead of allowing "engineering and economy to first define the object," says Kroll in *ARCH+* 77/1984, "the program starts with the existing landscape, then allows the new elements and their variants to be introduced, their connections to the surroundings checked and then visualized in a form explainable to non-specialists."[4]

The program does not just create an image from the design, it allows the user to gain an idea of the effect of the design in the given context in advance with the help of a digitally generated visualization. The starting point for this is a 3D wire model, which is then edited graphically on the computer:

> "Every building is individually pictured with CAD and then positioned on the layout. An in-house subprogram takes out 'all the guts' to leave only the contours and the buildings. Then the designer has a clear view of the corners of the surfaces and can apply color to them, which makes the lines behind the surfaces disappear from view and from the saved file."[5]

The result is a silhouetted, strongly rasterized representation that, despite the lack of an illumination model, succeeds in suggesting something like a landscape with symbolically modeled clouds in the sky, a small truck on the road, some trees, and an outline of mountains in the background. The image, therefore, highlights the dependency of the digital image on the conditions of its technical reproduction (→ Image 10). Lacking color, the black-and-white print in *ARCH+* loses some important information. This is in contrast to the color print in the French architectural journal *L'Architecture d'Aujourd'hui* in April 1986, where Kroll's program made its debut as a piece of software "which helps in achieving increasingly realistic and detailed simulations."[6] The comparison also showed that the image in the French publication had been cropped.

47

Image 7

7

Floyd Gillis

Advertising Animation
"ESPN City"
(Omnibus Computer
Graphics, 1985)

Rendering
Print of the image file
in: *Bauwelt*, 78, 1987,
1/2 (9 Jan.), p. 38

1   Kay Friedrichs, Günter Stöhr, and
    Gregor Wessels, "3D-CAD mit
    Solid Modeling" (CAD-Journal
    12), in *ARCH+*, 1987, 89 (May),
    pp. 12–13, here p. 12.

2   Kay Friedrichs and Gregor
    Wessels, "CAD Futures 1985
    in Delft" (CAD-Journal 5), in
    ARCH+, 1985, 82 (Oct.), p. 9.

3   With thanks to Floyd Gillis.

4   Mathias P. Hirche, "Technische
    Architekturdarstellung," in
    Bauwelt, 78, 1987, 1/2 (9 Jan.),
    pp. 46–51, here p. 51.

As well as design, visualization using the computer is another art brought into architectural practice from "the outside." In *ARCH+* 89/1987 it says: "Something particularly annoying is the missed opportunity to put today's exciting developments in the field of computer animation on existing CAD systems. […] As a rule, a perspective, 'primitive' wire model of the building is plotted then transferred by hand onto tracing paper and revised to make it […] easily understandable to the client."[1] What clearly shows here is the originally separate development of digital design and visualization tool technologies.

The examples of images from the US-American "superstars who, untroubled by financial constraints, […] come up with splendid results by any standard of drawing creation and visualization" therefore make an even greater impression and not only on the German public; however, "these exceptions aside, everything else is jam tomorrow."[2] Such images are demonstrations of what is possible, they are technically avant-garde examples that do not even remotely reflect the practice of architectural representation in Germany at the end of the 1980s.

This image from *Bauwelt* 1/2/1987 "Blicke und Bilder" also shows the current methods and techniques of architectural representation. What cannot be seen, however, as indicated in the image caption, is the "simulated city district provided as a design aid," but a freeze-frame from a computer-animated advertising film, which had been created by Floyd Gillis from Omnibus Computer Graphics, New York, for the US-American sports station ESPN. The film consists of rendered individual images shown at a frequency of thirty images per second, which were saved on a diskette and put together on an Ampex video machine for animation in the analog television signal. It was already possible to integrate scanned photographs and even video film sequences into the rendering process. Freeze-frames like these were, on the other hand, photographed on 35 mm slide film from the computer screen.[3] The adjacent image shows the printed-out digitalized version of an analog slide from the screenshot of a digitally generated video film.

At that time, architectural offices in Germany are some distance away from having this equipment and these possibilities of computer graphics at hand for visualizing the projects. The digital techniques are available and well-known; however, for a majority of architects they are neither affordable nor practical. Mathias P. Hirche, Head of the Center for Model Simulation at TU Berlin, summarizes the status quo of digital architectural representation in the same issue as follows:

"The CAD systems for architects have up to now been suitable for three-dimensional representation only to a limited extent. […] The drawings amount to not much more than line drawings, and colored surfaces are a rare exception. Only very complex and expensive programs are able to differentiate between visible and hidden lines for perspective representations. The situation is different for programs for graphic artists and layouters. Computer-aided 'image composing' greatly extends the possibilities to levels of which the architecture CAD user could only dream. Moving, colored surface graphics are available for uneven surfaces. However, these programs do not have any specific architectural applications for this, therefore the colorful perspective is not yet easily accessible as a by-product of CAD for architects."[4]

49

Image 8

8

Heiko Lukas,
Ulrike Seifritz

Schinkel Competition 1987

Hand drawing
Print of the digital copy
Architectural Museum
of the TU Berlin,
Inv. No. SW-A 1987,
04–05

1   *Daidalos*, 1981, 1 (15 Sept.):
    "Die Zeichnung als Medium der
    Abstraktion"; Heinrich Klotz,
    "Die Architekturzeichnung als
    Medium einer neuen Ästhetik,"
    in *Jahrbuch für Architektur
    1981/1982*, Braunschweig and
    Wiesbaden 1981, pp. 150–51.

2   Werner Oechslin, "Editorial,"
    in *Daidalos*, 1987, 25 (15 Sept.):
    "Die verführerische Zeichnung,"
    p. 23.

3   "Berichte und Projekte" (*ARCH+*
    journal), in *ARCH+*, 1984, 77
    (Nov.), pp. 4–9, here p. 5.

4   Oechslin, "Editorial."

5   Werner Durth, "Gebrochene
    Spiegel: Reflexionen über
    einen Atelierbesuch bei Helmut
    Jacoby," in *Daidalos*, 1987,
    25 (15 Sept.), pp. 92–105,
    here p. 93.

6   Cf. e.g. *Bauwelt*, 78, 1987, 3
    (16 Jan.): "'Frankfurt-Projekte.'"

7   Cf. *Bauwelt*, 87, 1996, 13 (4 April),
    p. 797; *Bauwelt*, 104, 2013,
    19 (17 May), p. 16; *Bauwelt*, 110,
    2019, 9 (3 May), p. 41.

While the digital image in architectural journals during the 1980s remains a spectacular, exceptional occurrence, the drawing boom gathers speed. While in 1981 the architectural drawing may have still been thought of as a "medium of abstraction" and celebrated as a "medium of a new aesthetic"[1] (→ Image 2), six years later the talk is of a "new drawing cult [...], to which architecture—with exhibition design and the art trade following close behind—have returned after a period of long-held disinterest."[2] By 1984, an article in *ARCH+* had critically pointed it out as a "method of communicating a personality cult via drawings," with which the architect presents himself "as a brilliant creature of urban development."[3] The focus is now no longer only on the axonometric perspective as a genuine architectural form of representation, but on the "seductive drawing," the "beautifully presented, pictorially suggestive drawing as a form of specific architectural representation."[4] The axonometric perspective is now also said to have a "tendency toward the automation of drawing in demonstrative mystification of three-dimensionality," "as is now cultivated in the barely legible bottom view isometry," which is the reason "the demand for concretist drawings mediating between the architectural design and the assessment by clients, financiers, and the critical public is growing."[5]

The presentation drawing depicted here comes from the Schinkel competition in 1987, the same year in which the architectural discourse is all about the "new drawing cult." However, it would be hard to describe it as seductive, mystifying, or concrete. It is an analog perspective representation that, as a clear white line drawing on a black background, comes very close to the view displayed on computer screens, which are currently used in this inverted mode. The observer is inserted into the image by the presented view from the train driver's cab and their eyes are directed onto the station, which is the actual design object. The slight tilt of the horizon masterfully circumvents the static symmetry of the central perspective and creates a dynamic pictorial effect.

The image shows in an exemplary manner the artistic quality and high standard of a hand drawing used as a medium for design representation, as is also to be found at the same time in architectural journals.[6] The view of the building from a vehicle is an infrequent but recurring motif that continues to appear in later journals.[7]

The Evolution of the Digital Image

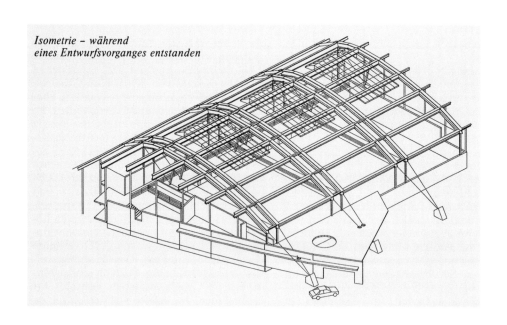

*Isometrie – während
eines Entwurfsvorganges entstanden*

Image 9

9

Unknown author

*CAD-drawn
Axonometric Projection*

CAD drawing
Reproduction of
journal image
in: *Bauwelt*, 79, 1988,
41 (28 Oct.), p. 1770

1 Fritz G. Schmidhäusler,
"CAD—Computer schlägt
Handarbeit" (CAD-Journal 4),
in *ARCH+*, 1985, 81 (Aug.), p. 9.
The following quote: ibid.

2 Hartmut Potreck worked for the
architects Schmidt-Schicketanz
in Munich at this time. With
thanks to Hartmut Potreck.
According to information kindly
supplied by Ulrike Braun of
Schmidt-Schicketanz Planer
GmbH, the drawing is no longer
unambiguously allocated to a
project.

3 Hartmut Potreck, "CAD-
Anwendung," in *Bauwelt*, 79,
1988, 41 (28 Oct.), pp. 1769–70,
1775, here p. 1769.

Even though creating plans and drawings with the computer initially requires almost as much effort and is nearly as protracted as creating them by hand, the advantages of computer-aided design soon become apparent. In 1985, according to *ARCH+*, the "quality of these drawings [...] can no longer be beaten by hand," because "time-consuming routine tasks such as the application of hatching are avoided [...] not to mention their precision and neatness (line accuracy)."[1] CAD offers an even greater lightening of the workload "when it comes to making amendments. There is no erasing or scratching off lines to do, and drawings need not be thrown away or started again from the beginning. Simply bring up the old drawing or part of it on the monitor, make the amendment—and plot the new drawing." The number of CAD drawings in the architectural journals rises with the increasing spread of the computer in architectural practice toward the end of the 1980s.

However, due to the similarity to hand-drawn axonometric projections, they are not easy to recognize, particularly since, as a rule, they are not declared as such in the journals. A comparison of the two shows the high standard and degree of perfection the hand-produced architectural drawing achieves. The differences occur mainly in the small to miniature details. With hand drawings, the distances between lines may vary, for example for repeating elements such as windows or glazing bars, or some lines may continue a little longer than they really need to. The indicators are slight inaccuracies with broken or parallel lines or in the geometric construction, where a line may be displaced or connects at a different angle.

So it is primarily the lower degree of precision that betrays the architectural drawing as a hand drawing. Computer-created and printed CAD drawings, on the other hand, are absolutely consistent. Their lines run perfectly parallel to one another, as is the case with curves and hatching. Overrunning, irregular lines, and other inaccuracies do not occur. They appear extremely functional and austere and have the character of a construction drawing.

This CAD drawing is one of the first that can be identified as such even by the untrained eye, because of its context. It is taken from *Bauwelt* 41/1988 "Computer," the first *Bauwelt* issue on this topic, which is published at the end of 1988, and appears in the article "CAD-Anwendung" by Hartmut Potreck.[2] As the author says in his report, the use of computers is above all targeted on "providing visualization support to allow design assumptions to be verified, including in the early stages of design"; CAD is hence seen mainly as a "production tool for the creation of drawings."[3] The digitally created drawing is therefore spoken of as an aid fulfilling an operative function in the design process. However, as a look through the journals at the end of the 1980s reveals, CAD drawings also fulfill representative functions.

The Evolution of the Digital Image

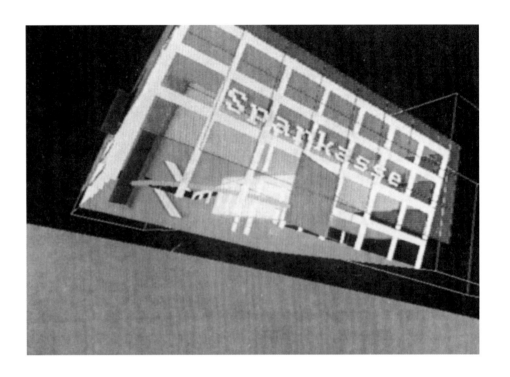

Image 10

10

Zechner & Zechner

Competition—Sparkasse Leoben (with Nicole Weber)

Rendering
Reproduction of
journal image
in: *ARCH+*, 1988, 96/97
(Nov./Dec.), p. 53

1   [Christoph and Martin Zechner],
    "De-Konstruktion per Computer.
    Wettbewerb Sparkasse Leoben,"
    in *ARCH+*, 1988, 96/97 (Nov./
    Dec.), pp. 52–53, here p. 52.
    All quotations there.

2   With thanks to Christoph
    Zechner.

3   With kind thanks to the
    Zechner & Zechner Vienna office
    for making the material available.

At the end of 1988, it is happening: the appearance of this picture marks the start of the regular entry of the digital image into architectural journals. It is the first fully digital representation, the first completely computer-created image that was not intended for purely demonstration purposes or included in a special issue, but an actual design from current architectural practice, presented to the public for the first time. It is the picture in which the digital image is first used in practice as a medium of design visualization in the journals.

The picture is part of a series of four images about a competition design that appear under the title "De-Konstruktion per Computer" in *ARCH+* 96/97 "Dekonstruktive Architektur."[1] The design was developed using utility software written in-house that allows users to generate "rooms, building components, shreds" by "intervening and controlling random processes […] within selected limits." However, the computer is also used "completely conventionally, e.g. for producing presentation images": "With the help of small transformation programs, data that had, for example, been saved on an IBM PC AT using AutoCAD could be transferred to an Amiga and further edited. The output, consisting of slides, hard copies or videos, is processed by programs such as Video-scape or Sculpt 3D on a Commodore Amiga."

As the image shows, the visualization appears highly schematic and abstract. The design is represented from an extreme bottom view so that the observer can look to a certain extent from below into the apparently floating building. The resulting perspective distortions make the architectural elements that are actually tilted difficult to recognize as such. The representation is specifically and obviously dynamized in order to suggest that the building is similarly invigorated. It can be said that the picture does not contribute to a better understanding of the actual building design. In the text accompanying the picture it also says: "for an easier understanding and the reasons for conformity to common ways of seeing, the images are conventionally drawn out by hand." Here this refers to elevation, plan, and section, which are printed as line drawings in the normal manner directly adjacent to the rendered perspectives. The focus is less on achieving the most realistic reproduction of the building and much more on emphasizing the design idea of the "De-Konstruktion" using digital visualization. Thus the renderings take the design to the edge of the current architecture movement that is also the theme of the journal.

These types of "computer images," as they are called here, are an absolute exception at this time in the journals. As a rule, designs are depicted as combinations of drawings and model photographs. As with "ESPN City" (→ Image 7), photography certainly plays its part here as well. The image clearly shows the raster pattern of the cathode ray tube monitor from which the digital visualization was photographed on slide film to provide photographic prints for the design office and printer's copies for reproductions.[2] This highlights the fundamental problem of the technical reproducibility of the digital image (→ Image 6), which drags on into the 1990s and is usually resolved in a practical way by means of analog photographs of monitor screens. As was the case with the image by Lucien Kroll, it came as a surprise, going by the photographic prints received, that the original of the picture printed in *ARCH+* turns out to have been in color.[3]

55

The Evolution of the Digital Image

Image 11

11

Zumtobel AG Dornbirn

Cophography with the Lighting Simulation Program COPHOS 2.0

Rendering
Reproduction of
journal image
in: *Bauwelt*, 80, 1989,
27 (14 July), p. 1309

1   Marian Behaneck, "Rechner-gestützte Darstellungsverfahren," in Marian Behaneck, Dieter J. Heimlich, and Peter Wossnig, *Vom CAAD zum Bild. Architektur als fotorealistische Erlebniswelt*, Neustadt a. d. W. 1991, pp. 43–130, here p. 67.

2   Ibid., p. 108.

3   BCH, "Was ist eigentlich Cophographie?," in *Bauwelt*, 80, 1989, 27 (14 July), p. 1309.

4   "Cophographie," in *ARCH+*, 1988, 96/97 (Nov./Dec.), pp. 106–7, here p. 106.

5   With thanks to Peter Dehoff, Head of the COPHOS program at Zumtobel Lighting GmbH in Dornbirn since 1987.

6   Behaneck, "Rechnergestützte Darstellungsverfahren," p. 116.

Architects such as Boullée and Le Corbusier earlier explored the relationship between light effects and architecture. In the same way, staging with light is a central aspect of architectural representation. This is very evident with digital architectural visualizations that have to thank the "simulation of natural lighting situations" as the main contributor to their photorealistic effect.[1] In addition to mapping, the projection of diverse patterns on surfaces, the representation of light is one of the significant roles of rendering. Starting with a simplified 3D model of the view of the planned building, the surfaces are given colors and textures to suggest the intended materialities (→ Image 6). With the help of specific graphics programs or modules, the model can then be staged with appropriate illumination by defining a light source (→ Image 5). The light intensity, light effects, or the influence of diffuse, indirect light on the object are aligned one upon the other. There are various illumination models available, such as Gouraud shading, ray tracing, or radiosity, which have their own different "photorealistic qualities."[2]

On the other hand, this illustration demonstrates the possibilities of representing light using the computer in the field of lighting design, which also plays a significant role in the architectural realization process. It was created using the COPHOS 2.0 simulation software developed by Zumtobel AG in Dornbirn, which allowed the users to "simulate lighting effects on the computer monitor that earlier would have required complex prototype models," and "arrive at an accurate image of the later effect using precise lighting design calculations which take into account all the surfaces of the object and the surroundings."[3] The program received a lot of coverage in the media because it "simulated light effects to a level of reality that had been previously unachievable."[4] The purpose of COPHOS is not to represent architecture but rather to create physically correct simulations of the real illumination interactions that would prevail later on the built structure.[5] As with "ESPN City" (→ Image 7), this example demonstrates the compositional possibilities of computer graphics in a non-architectural field and with that also brings home to the public its potential for architectural visualization. However, therein lies the fundamental difference, in that visualization software, specifically rendering programs, "as a rule use their own lighting models that do not exactly conform with the rules of physics."[6] Renderings do not simulate light; they imitate it as an aesthetic means of creating highly photorealistic image effects.

The illustration is one of only two digital images that appear in any of the issues of *Bauwelt* in 1989.

The Evolution of the Digital Image

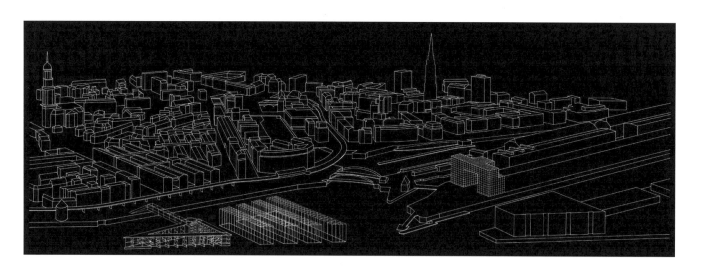

Image 12

12

Karl Hufnagel,
Michael Rafaelian

Schinkel Competition 1989

Hand drawing
Print of the digital copy
Architectural Museum
of the TU Berlin,
Inv. No. SW-St 1989,
03–01

1   The "Architekten Computer
    Systeme" trade fair initiated by
    the Hesse Chamber of Architects
    first took place from November
    30 to December 2, 1984, in
    Wiesbaden. See *Bauwelt*, 75,
    1984, 44 (23 Nov.), p. 1869.

2   Joachim Langner,
    "ACS-Messesplitter," in *Bauwelt*,
    80, 1989, 9 (24 Feb.), pp. 332–34,
    here p. 334. Template books
    were a useful resource for
    drawing practice, for example
    Larry Evans's *Bildvorlagen-Atlas
    für Architekten, Grafiker und
    Illustratoren; maßstäblich,
    vielfältig, aktuell*, Wiesbaden and
    Berlin 1987.

3   Ibid. Also in *Bauwelt*, 84, 1993,
    42 (5 Nov.), p. 2300 ("Die letzte
    Seite").

4   Klaus Hüttner, "CAD—Automa-
    tisation in der Bauplanung,"
    in *CAD: Architektur automatisch?*
    (Bauwelt Fundamente, 76), ed.
    Walter Ehlers, Gernot Feldhusen,
    and Carl Steckeweh, Braun-
    schweig and Wiesbaden 1986,
    pp. 131–43, here p. 136.

The first graphical results created with the computer, such as those that emerge in the architectural journals around the mid-1980s, are extremely similar in appearance to the widely seen hand-drawn axonometric projections and are quite often edited by hand (→ Image 4). As made clear in a report about the ACS trade fair in *Bauwelt* from 1988,[1] even at the end of the 1980s it is "still usual practice to use the computer exclusively for the building, while the phlegmatic draftsman embellishes everything that goes with it, adding the usual greenery, little people, and fast sports cars 'freehand.'"[2] There is even software for "the 'real free-hand computer drawing'" that is intended to give the impression of a manually produced drawing by the artificial "blurring of the building's image."[3]

The already difficult task of distinguishing analog from digital architectural representations is made much more complicated by the technical perfection of the computer drawing clearly exercising such a fascination (→ Image 9) that the plotter style begins to influence the drawing style (→ Image 3). Klaus Hüttner had said three years before:

"The form of representation is obviously subject to the rules and principles of the tools used to create the images—refined by contemporary taste. Sometimes this borders on a farce. For example, architectural drawings may look as if they were produced by the computer, however, on closer inspection the small shortcomings of traditional hand-drawing tools cannot be concealed."[4]

Hand-drawn and computer drawings come to resemble one another in terms of their graphical appearance toward the end of the 1980s and converge in certain respects such that it is all the more difficult to distinguish between them.

In the case of this example as well, it is not easy to say with certainty whether the urban perspective of the Hamburg harbor district, with its fine, accurate white lines on black background, is a computer-generated representation or a deliberate imitation of the stylistic features of a computer graphic. The degree of accuracy achieved is certainly impressive. At the same time, the reversal of the conventional choice of colors is again suggestive of a CAD drawing effect. The good level of readability this creates is further improved in the foreground of the image where the actual design stands by changing the line thickness and increasing the amount of detail. Because curved lines, like those on the bowstring truss bridge, the cupola of St. Michael's, and the elevated section of the U3 metro, are represented as true curves and not as graduated polygons (→ Image 5), it can be assumed that this is a hand drawing. Even though it was possible to create a curve out of many short chords with CAD at the time, it does not look as if these curves have been drawn that way.

59

The Evolution of the Digital Image

Image 13

13

ART+COM e.V.

Simulation Potsdamer Platz Subway Station, Berlin

Rendering
Reproduction of
journal image
in: *Bauwelt*, 81, 1990,
17 (4 May), p. 867

1   Irina Davidovici, "Grenzen
    ausloten. Architektur in den
    1990er-Jahren," in *ARCH+*, 2017,
    229 (July), pp. 70–73, here p. 70.

2   Dieter Hoffmann-Axthelm,
    "Ausfahrt Potsdamer Platz,"
    in *Bauwelt*, 81, 1990, 17 (4 May),
    pp. 864–67, here p. 864.

3   Ibid., p. 866.

4   Thomas Wagner, "Terravision:
    Die ganze Erde im Blick" <https://
    ndion.de/de/terravision-die-
    ganze-erde-im-blick/> (last
    accessed 24.1.2024).

5   rola, "Sterile Welten," *taz*
    dated 23.4.1990 <https://taz.de/
    STERILEWELT/!1771142/>
    (last accessed 24.1.2024).

6   Hoffmann-Axthelm, "Aus-
    fahrt Potsdamer Platz," p. 866.

7   See rola, "Sterile Welten."

The 1990s mark more than one epochal political and societal turning point. Architecture as well stands at the "beginning of a borderless era with borderless possibilities,"[1] which is later reflected in the journals. In the 1990s, all the earlier developments in drawing during the previous decade arising from the digitalization of design and, in terms of approach, visualization techniques are widely seen in practice, and their use advances at a rapid pace.

This specific historic situation also has a bearing on this image. Published in issue 17 in spring 1990, a few months after the fall of the Berlin Wall, it is the first regular digital architectural image not intended for demonstration purposes to appear in *Bauwelt* and is the counterpart to → Image 10 in *ARCH+*. The drawing is not intended to be a forerunner of a future design but to visualize a historic situation.

The context of the image is an article by Dieter Hoffmann-Axthelm on the urban design character of Potsdamer Platz in the "twenties, […] the place with the most vehicular traffic in Europe; in the time of the wall, the place of greatest traffic silence."[2] The author argues that, in view of the present dystopian character of the place, an image of its earlier state lost through war and division should first be made in order to avoid the risk of creating an "ode to white-collar culture with dead silence after 5 pm"[3] as a result of over-hasty replanning.

The article is accompanied by a series of seven visualizations of the Potsdamer Platz subway station created by the Berlin studio ART+COM—Forschungs- und Entwicklungszentrum für rechnergestütztes Gestalten e. V., "an agency closely related to the Chaos Computer Club for people interested in art, science and hacking."[4] It was founded in 1988 as a research and development center for computer-aided design as part of a "research project into data communication between the Schools of Art and Design at Berlin, Braunschweig and Kassel."[5] As the picture caption suggests, the visualization is based on the assumption

> "that the 'roots' of the square, in the depths of the still-present subway stations, will be the point of departure for the design concepts of the development options for the long-unused parcels of land. Because these stations had been closed to the public since 1961, they had largely vanished from the consciousness of the planners and decision-making committees. Using computer simulations, these buildings can he brought to life again and made visible in the sense of collecting evidence at an archaeological scene of crime.'"[6]

The image shows an artificial lighting situation produced by ray tracing in which the light paths are intended to give a realistic impression, but the surfaces do not quite integrate with one another. The image composition is the same as that of a photographic snapshot, which points to it being based on a freeze-frame from a computer animation.[7] The unretouched small hairs and particles of dust, which can be seen clearly in the picture, indicate that analog photography has also played a part here.

61

Image 14

14

Bertelsmann & Partner

*Project Alexander Galleries
Berlin Buildings 1–7*

Rendering
Reproduction of
journal image
in: *Bauwelt*, 82, 1991,
39 (18 Oct.), p. 2102

1 For more information about this
and the associated quantitative
information, see Fig. 1 in the
contribution by Florian Henrich,
p. 33.

2 Joachim Langner, "Architekt
und Computer," in *Bauwelt*, 81,
1990, 2/3 (19 Jan.), pp. 116–19,
here p. 117.

3 David Wakefield, "Tensyl—Ein in-
teraktives Grafik-CAD-System für
Entwurf und Zuschnitt leichter
Flächentragwerke," in *ARCH+*,
1991, 107 (Mar.), pp. 79–81,
here p. 81.

4 Ibid.

5 Langner, "Architekt und
Computer," p. 118.

6 Joachim Langner, "Architekten
Computer auf den Spuren
der Salier," in *Bauwelt*, 82,
1991, 10 (8 Mar.), pp. 456–57,
here p. 457.

7 Wakefield, "Tensyl," p. 81.

8 Langner, "Architekt und
Computer," p. 117.

9 Langner, "Architekten Computer,"
p. 457.

10 Marian Behaneck, "Rechner-
gestützte Darstellungsverfahren,"
in Marian Behaneck, Dieter J.
Heimlich, and Peter Wossnig,
*Vom CAAD zum Bild. Architektur
als fotorealistische Erlebniswelt*,
Neustadt a. d. W. 1991,
pp. 43–130, here p. 129.

11 Ibid., p. 125.

The year 1991, for the first time, sees a moderate but nevertheless sig-nificant rise in the number of digital images appearing in *Bauwelt*.[1] This increase can be attributed on the one hand to the advancing technologi-cal developments and on the other hand to the building boom emerging in the wake of German reunification. The illustration shown here is one of about a dozen renderings in total that appeared in journals over the course of that year. At the same time, the small number of examples shows that the use of the digital architectural image is still anything but a matter of course, even at the start of the 1990s. Fully digital represen-tations like these are very much an exception in the journals.

That the computer is hardly used as a visualization tool in archi-tectural practice at this time is evident from statements such as "the architect spends one morning per year at the most working on 'com-puter screen painting'"[2] and "even once these images are created on the screen, there is still the problem of printing out the hard copy in comparable quality."[3] In a nutshell, nothing has changed: making analog "photos directly from the computer screen," converting "RGB computer signals into slides," or "turning images on the monitor into video films" continues to be a very expensive option.[4] Although the first printers are available, either they are "in the Porsche super-league"[5] in terms of price or their quality is sufficient "only for quite modest demands."[6]

At the same time, it is predicted that the future "developments in computer graphics [...] would go in the direction of the production of photorealistic illustrations with improved hardware implementation for ray tracing and radiosity visualizations."[7] Whereas earlier, "strange iso-metric projections or wire perspectives flickered on most monitors,"[8] to-day, the flickering image is "no longer green or orange as it was then but is now multicolored with solid surfaces"—and the keyword is mentioned here as well: "These images are called photorealism."[9]

Against the background of this situation, it becomes clear that digital images like these achieve a somewhat pioneering status, which is awarded here purely because of the colors—the first regular color ren-dering in *Bauwelt*. The unnatural lighting situation with its high contrast of light and shadow and the deep placement of the light source creates a three-dimensional effect. Transparency is employed as well, as can be seen in the foreground near the purple parts of the buildings. There is a clear schematic character to the representation, in which the design appears like a model. Details are not reproduced. "Photorealism" in this image essentially amounts to the representation of color under the ef-fect of light and shadow.

Despite the limitations of the medium, the appearance of visuali-zations initiated the "appeal of the new, the spectacular";[10] the "image-promoting effect"[11] of these images is huge.

63

Image 15

15

Gemeentewerken
Rotterdam

*Design Kop van Zuid
Rotterdam*

Illustration: Cas Schook;
Photography: Dick
Sellenraad (Aeroview)
Analog photography
with airbrush markings
Reproduction of
journal image
in: *Bauwelt*, 83, 1992,
4 (24 Jan.), p. 153

1   With thanks to Mattijs van
    Ruijven, Head Urban Planner,
    City Development Rotterdam.

2   With thanks to Cas Schook.

3   With thanks to Lonneke Visser of
    the Rotterdam Stadsarchief for
    making available a color print.

4   See Mathias P. Hirche, "Tech-
    nische Architekturdarstellung,"
    in *Bauwelt*, 78, 1987, 1/2 (9 Jan.),
    pp. 46–51, here p. 51.

5   Jens Guthoff, "Architekturgrafik
    mit CAD" (*ARCH+*-Baumarkt), in
    ARCH+, 1990, 102 (Jan.), p. 89.

6   "Software" (*ARCH+*-Baumarkt),
    in: *ARCH+*, 1992, 112 (June), p. 92.

In contrast to the rudimentary photorealism of the first renderings, this illustration looks so realistic that it could be mistaken for a photograph while leafing through the pages. Only on closer inspection and with the knowledge that the pictured structure, the Erasmus Bridge in Rotterdam, did not exist at that time does it become obvious that it is a manipulated photograph. Only the transparent high-rise buildings in the Kop van Zuid former harbor district give rise to the suspicion that the image was edited by computer. However, it turns out from the research that a computer was never involved. In the archives of the Rotterdam urban development department, a PDF flyer containing the illustration[1] names the photographer as well as Cas Schook, the illustrator. After contact was made, it was learned that the transparency effect was done with an airbrush.[2] Even on the scanned color original from 1991, the spray paint applied to the photograph can be identified only with difficulty.[3]

This example makes clear in an understandable way that it can be quite difficult, even in the case of architectural representation practice during the 1990s, to distinguish between digital and analog images. The following general rule could apply to the 1990s: it is probable that a computer is involved, but it is sometimes difficult to be certain whether or how it plays a part.

The image therefore represents a development in visualization that had already started in the 1980s[4] and could be described as a successive hybridization of the customary analog representation process. This is primarily considered to be the increasing enhancement of the photomontage with digital image elements (→ Image 21) as an affordable and practical alternative to costly and complex rendering, as described in 1990 in *ARCH+*:

"The rationalization and further development of formalized drawing gain in significance as experience in using CAD increases. Two trends are present here: one is the efforts made to increase the legibility of the representation; the second is to bring more atmosphere into a formalized representation. [...] Today's state of the technology includes so-called photorealistic representations, [...] which the layperson cannot distinguish from photographs. The amount of effort is considerable [...] What cannot be seen, the atmosphere, the situation, is seldom perceived. More realism and vitality can be achieved by using a montage of images of a building created by a computer in a photograph of its surroundings previously imported into the computer."[5]

It is a significant coincidence that the term *Photoshop* emerges in the journals during the same year. The "program for professional retouching and further processing of color images and half-tone originals" has been available since 1990 and, according to *ARCH+*, is of interest in the field of architectural presentation "because of its various effects functions with which the rendered presentation drawings can be further processed."[6]

65

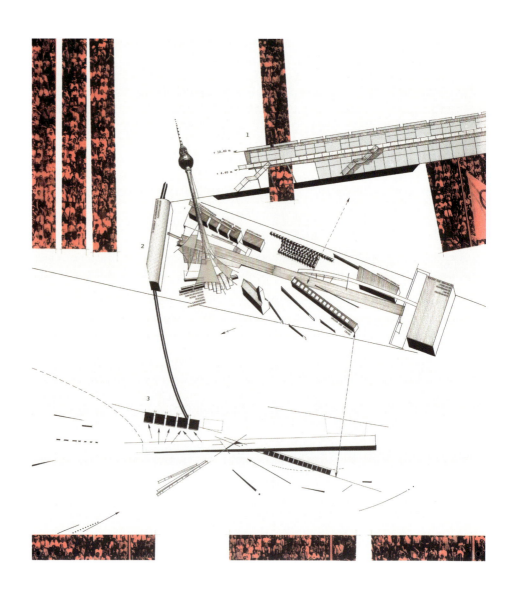

Image 16

16

Charles de Picciotto

Schinkel Competition 1992

Analog collage
Print of the digital copy
Architectural Museum
of TU Berlin,
Inv. No. SW-A 1992,
01–03

1   See Martino Stierli, *Montage and the Metropolis: Architecture, Modernity, and the Representation of Space*, New Haven and London 2018, ch. 3: "Photomontage in Architectural Representation," pp. 80–125, here p. 81.

2   See Mathias P. Hirche, "Technische Architekturdarstellung," in *Bauwelt*, 78, 1987, 1/2 (9 Jan.), pp. 46–51, here pp. 49–50.

3   Suada is the goddess of persuasion in Roman mythology. See *Herder Lexikon Griechische und römische Mythologie*, Freiburg, Basel, and Vienna 1990, p. 207.

4   See Stierli, *Montage and the Metropolis*, pp. 18–20.

5   *Die Fotomontage. Geschichte und Wesen einer Kunstform*, exhib. cat., Ingolstadt 1969.

6   See e.g. the *Hamburger Handels, Industrie und Gewerbe-Adreßbuch 1930*, pp. 340–41 or the advertising section in *Wasmuths Monatshefte für Baukunst*, 16, 1932, 1 (Jan.), p. VII.

The principle of the photomontage as a specific form of design visualization will become digitalized during the 1990s (→ Image 21). Its appearances in the journals can be traced back to around 1900.[1] The results of drawing on photographs can be found, for example, in the work of Friedrich von Thiersch, such as in his 1902 design for the new assembly room building at a health resort in Wiesbaden. Gluing suitably trimmed model photographs, adjusted to provide an adequate perspective, into previously taken photographs of the surroundings of the existing site for the proposed building is also described as a photomontage[2] and can be seen in *Bauwelt* and *ARCH+* well beyond the 1990s. All these various forms are based on the common aim: to present the architectural design visually through the medium of the photograph. In fact this is an impossibility, because the designed object does not exist in real form and, as a consequence, cannot be photographed. The purpose of the photomontage as a process of design representation is to create this effect. Its main principle is objective simulation, based on the supposed objectivity of the photographic reproduction of reality. In this respect, the photomontage comes close to achieving a persuasive moment.[3] However, it seeks to convince the observer that they are looking at a photograph of a real building, although it does not yet exist.

On the other hand, this image, with its free combination of plan, axonometric projection, and elevation, together with lines, arrows, text, and strips of cut-up photographs of a crowd scene with a swaying and dancing ensemble, refers to another modern graphic tradition: the collage, which stretches back to the avant-garde movements of the 1910s.[4] No claim to being a highly realistic simulation is raised here. This form of design representation is much more a self-contained aesthetic pictorial language. Certainly, the conceptual difference between collage and montage is not always clear, because the photomontage has the "history and nature of an art form."[5]

Like the photomontage, the collage undergoes digitalization in the 1990s (→ Image 22). What is meant here by collage is primarily an aesthetic pictorial form of architectural representation, which experiences a boom as a genre sui generis around 2000 (→ Image 25), while a montage in the context of this book is primarily a technical process that can be traced back to the time of the Weimar Republic as offers of photographic services in the advertising sections of journals.[6]

67

The Evolution of the Digital Image

Image 17

17

Jean Nouvel, Emmanuel Cattani et Associés

Friedrichstadt-Passagen Berlin Block 207

Rendering
Print of the image file
in: *Bauwelt*, 84, 1993,
21 (28 May), p. 1118

1   Peter Rumpf, "Die
    Friedrichstadt-Passagen in
    Berlin Mitte," in *Bauwelt*, 82,
    1991, 18/19 (17 May), pp. 972–77,
    here p. 976.

2   Martina Düttmann, "Die neue
    Friedrichstraße," in *Bauwelt*, 84,
    1993, 21 (28 May), pp. 1108–27,
    here p. 1118.

3   Cf. text → Image 3 and 33.

In the same way as "ESPN City" (→ Image 7) brought home to the public the possibilities of computer graphics for creating architectural representations in the 1980s, this image shows the progressive approach of French architects in the area of digital visualization of design at the start of the 1990s.

It is the first of a series of four digital images from the first half of the 1990s that are presented here (→ Image 17 to 20). They are notable not just for the particular way they have been represented but for their rarity value alone in the context of journals. They are not typical of the great majority of developments in the field of visualization.

In the 1990s, the story of developments in visualization in journals is largely still about analog images. The practice of architectural representation is extremely diverse. It includes graphics, drawings, presentation images, model photographs as well as montages, collages, and endoscopies. The digital image, on the other hand, appears only seldom and sporadically. It is sneaking into current visualization practice, as it were. Its entry advances little by little and intermittently—a process extending over the whole of the 1990s. Digital architectural images start appearing as CAD line drawings, as colored CAD drawings intended for presentation, as fully digital images, digital photomontages, and manipulated photographs, then finally as digital collages, mostly in small formats and seldom in color. The predominant image medium used for design visualization in the journals of the 1990s is without doubt the analog model photograph.

Images such as these therefore stand out even more. The qualitative leap compared with the earlier status quo of digital architectural representation in the journals is significant. The design of the Berlin branch of the French department store chain Galeries Lafayette was published in 1991 in *Bauwelt*, where it is characterized as a "closed volume, playing with natural and artificial light" and "reflecting the light internally and externally off its facades by multimedia effects."[1] While the design representation is still purely analog, achieved using model photographs, graphics, and drawings, rendering is now intended to visually communicate the specific design theme of "'light projections, messages and images.'"[2]

By exploiting to the maximum the technological possibilities of rendering, the image anticipates the gleaming light effect with the help of transparency effects. Not only is it possible to employ transparency extensively, it is also done in a range of different ways. A number of reflective and lustrous effects are designed to create a glistening, shiny situation in daylight, while at the same time allowing views into the building's interior. The composition, including skillful repetition of the various silhouettes of people, and the random-looking partial images on the left and right edges, allows the representation to give an initial impression of a photograph, which is reinforced by the added background photograph of the cloudy blue sky. To produce this type of rendering requires the sort of financial means and technical capabilities available at this point in time only to large architectural firms.[3] A certain slight blurring and not least the film transport strips that can be seen in the untrimmed scan point to this image being a reproduction of an analog photograph of a computer monitor screen.

69

The Evolution of the Digital Image

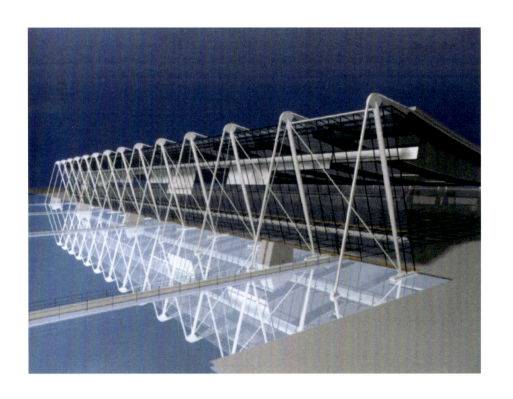

Image 18

18

AS+P Albert Speer + Partner

EXPO 2000 Hannover Messe Hall

Rendering
Print of the image file
in: *Bauwelt*, 85, 1994,
42 (4 Nov.), p. 2349

1   SR, "[Editorial]," in *Bauwelt*, 85,
     1994, 20 (20 May), p. 1073.

2   Johannes Dell, "Im CAD-Zirkel,"
     in *Bauwelt*, 85, 1994, 42 (4 Nov.),
     pp. 2346–53, here p. 2352.

3   Ibid., p. 2349.

4   Ibid., p. 2353.

5   Ibid., p. 2346.

As is clear from the journals, the "image-promoting effect" of the digital image in architecture in the first half of the 1990s also attracts some critical reactions. Instead of dying down during this time, the "appeal of the new, the spectacular" appears to have become even more hyped around the digital image as a medium for architectural representation. In 1994, *Bauwelt* supposes the beginning of "an age of abundance of all varieties of architectural presentation images" and therefore "the path to the anonymous architecture imaging machine appears preprogrammed and irreversible."[1] However, if the excitement about the computer is as expressed in statements like these, it stands in curious contrast to architectural practice.

This discrepancy is also a subject in a report by Johannes Dell from the architectural practice Albert Speer und Partner. The report is published at the end of 1994 in the second *Bauwelt* special issue on the topic of the computer with the title "CAD as CAD can" and includes the image opposite. It reveals that the computer is used in two ways for visualization in architectural offices, namely as a "design tool for checking three-dimensional integrity and for presentation purposes."[2] However, in the "architectural journals […] much more space is devoted to 3D animation than it deserves, based on its actual significance to the architect's day-to-day life in the design office."[3] In fact, according to Dell, the "requirement that architects must offer increasingly more attractive 3D animations than the latest state of the technology, […] was promoted by the software manufacturers themselves—in their advertising and informational literature."[4] The author goes on to say:

> "It has since come to be said that the software manufacturers are helpful to their architectural customers in their products, e.g. for the upgrading of simple wire models to smart-looking 3D presentation drawings using complex rendering. Thus the impression emerges that these drawings are being created, as it were, almost in passing and are now a natural part of everyday architectural design work. As a rule, it is hardly ever mentioned how much work and know-how is invested in a well-produced 3D simulation, and how seldom there is enough time available in a project schedule to create one. […] Of course, it is completely normal practice to have presentation drawings completed by 'external' agencies."[5]

In contrast, this illustration is an internally produced presentation image, which is part of the design for a hall at EXPO 2000 in Hanover. The chosen form of representation presents the design less as a building and more as an object. It employs a compositional technique from photography: the reflection in the water in front of the object creates an optical double of the architecture. The higher-than-usual camera position adopted for the image makes it appear that the observer is floating in midair. This not only achieves an imposing pictorial effect but also shows off the slender supporting structure of the hall. That being said, the representation takes the observer to the edge of confusion. The aim here is less to attempt to create a photorealistic representation and more to present a schematic clarification of the engineering structure forming the main element of the design. The slight blurriness of the image suggests also in this case it is an analog photograph of a computer monitor screen.

71

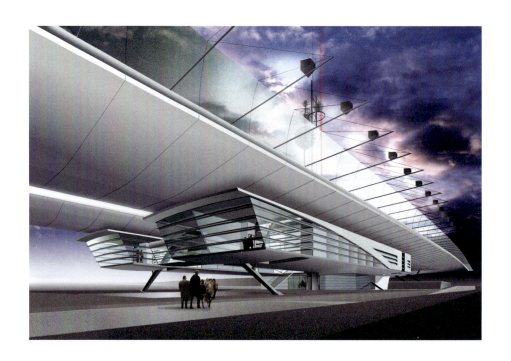

Image 19

19

Odile Decq &
Benoît Cornette

*A14 Freeway Control
Center, Nanterre*

Rendering
Print of the image file
in: *Bauwelt*, 86, 1995,
31 (18 Aug.), p. 1690

1   Stan Allen, "Endgeschwindig-
    keiten: Der Computer im
    Entwurfs-Studio," in *ARCH+*,
    1995, 128 (Sept.), pp. 58–62,
    here p. 59. Further quotations in
    the sentence: ibid.

2   Cf. Winfried Nerdinger (ed.),
    *Die Architekturzeichnung.
    Vom barocken Idealplan zur
    Axonometrie*, Munich 1986.

3   Cf. text → Image 2 and 3.

4   Cf. text → Image 40.

5   Cf. text → Image 15.

6   Andreas Ruby, "Abgehängt.
    Autobahnkontrollzentrum und
    Hochstraße A14 in Nanterre," in
    Bauwelt, 86, 1995, 31 (18 Aug.),
    pp. 1690–93, here p. 1693.

7   Ibid.

Amid the hype about the digital image as a medium for architectural representation, what appears to be the first conspicuous critique on photorealistic rendering is published in *ARCH+* 128/1995 "Architektur in Bewegung—Entwerfen am Computer," the third *ARCH+* issue on digitalization in architectural practice. According to Stan Allen, "the peculiar aspects of digital technology [...] is the evaluation of a new realism. From Hollywood special effects to architectural photorealistic representation, the success of the new technology is measured in terms of its ability to seamlessly reproduce reality."[1] In architecture, this becomes "clear in the techniques of visualization," where "computer technology promises to create ever more realistic simulations." However, "this ignores what traditionally gives architectural representation its immense conceptualization power—namely the necessary degree of abstraction, the distance between the thing and its representation."

Allen formulates here one of the main accusations against the photorealism of the digital architectural image, which will subsequently come up time and time again (→ Image 46) and regularly appears in the history of architectural representation as a traditional argument in the pair of opposites: abstraction and vividness,[2] as last happened with the "reartification" of architecture at the beginning of the 1980s.[3]

A search for a similar type of illustration in the same year's issues of *ARCH+* and *Bauwelt* shows, on the one hand, that the digital image continues to appear only rarely. On the other, it becomes clear that judging what is "photorealistic" obviously changes with the progress of the technical means of representation.[4]

Hence, today's judges would hardly say this rendering had the "ability to seamlessly reproduce reality." Measured against the quality standards of its day, however, it is certainly an ambitious representation that stands out in the context of reproduction practice in the journals at that time, not least because of its rarity value. As the staffage, the dramatic clouds in the sky, and the antenna mast reveal, the principle of the digital montage has already been employed here to integrate digitalized photographic image elements into the rendering.[5] Glass is shown as transparent, allowing views into the building. Reflecting the building type, which "in all its parts is the result of close cooperation between architect and engineer,"[6] the computer representation is intended to emphasize the technologically advanced nature of the design as a "realization of speed in architecture."[7] The scene appears at the same time abstract and unreal instead of realistic and true to reality. Although the building is located correctly in the space as far as perspective is concerned, without integration into the context, it appears to float like a UFO through time and space.

The Evolution of the Digital Image

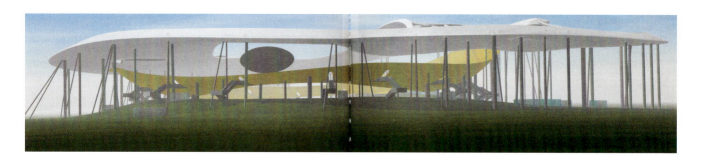

Image 20

20

Peter Kulka with
Ulrich Königs

*Sports Stadium Chemnitz
2002*

Rendering
Reproduction of
journal image
in: *Bauwelt*, 87, 1996,
12 (29 Mar.), pp. 730/731

1   Cecil Balmond, "Informeller
    Diskurs über die Konstruktion,"
    in *ARCH+*, 1996, 131 (April),
    pp. 34–39, here p. 35.

2   Ibid., p. 34.

3   Peter Kulka and Ulrich Königs,
    "Sportstadion Chemnitz 2002,"
    in *Bauwelt*, 87, 1996, 12 (29 Mar.),
    pp. 728–33, here p. 729. The
    image was created by Martin
    Schikulski, Motion Unlimited,
    Düsseldorf, see p. 733.

4   Balmond, "Informeller Diskurs,"
    p. 39.

5   Ibid., p. 37.

6   Kulka and Königs, "Sportstadion
    Chemnitz 2002," p. 728.

7   Ibid., p. 730.

In architectural image practice as reflected in the journals, computer visualizations appear around the middle of the 1990s as an advertisement for modernity and a sign of technological progressiveness. They are used not only because of their specific aesthetic qualities but also for their ability to symbolize and signal. On the one hand, these visualizations are expected to show that the architectural office involved is accomplished in the use of the very latest technology, while on the other, they express the innovative character of the design through an appropriately advanced type and method of representation. As can be seen with the two previous examples, renderings are therefore frequently used for engineering structures. That may be one of the reasons for the sharp rise in the number of digital images appearing in *Bauwelt* from the beginning of the second half of the 1990s and the maintenance of that higher level through to the turn of the millennium.

This is also the case with this visualization of the stadium design by Peter Kulka with Ulrich Königs and the London engineering consultancy Ove Arup & Partners submitted with the bid for the 2002 European Athletics Championship in Chemnitz, which is presented both in *Bauwelt* and in *ARCH+*. At the start of this "novel, informally shaped stadium concept,"[1] which was developed "in opposition to the requirements of conventional stadium architecture,"[2] the architects first had in mind "a specific visual effect which would then be created with an appropriate structure."[3] The concept is based on the idea of "the naturalness of a 'cloud' and a 'wood' combined with the artificiality of columns and a roof"[4] realized in a flowing, open form, free "from any kind of concentric influences,"[5] which dissolves the "difference between inside and outside" and removes "any aggressiveness from the building."[6]

While numerous photographic close-up pictures of the model are intended to suggest the subjective experience of the architecture from the viewpoint of the stadium spectators, it is the task of the ambitious, compositional rendering to make clear the specific design concept in the form of a presentation image. Instead of photorealism, the image is a simplified schematic representation reduced to four principal elements of the design: the relaxed combination of the artificial hill, the spectator stands, the forest of supporting columns, and the translucent roof membrane. Every element in the image has its own assigned color, which has been chosen on the principle of local color: green, yellow, gray, white, and blue for the sky. The viewpoint at human eye height allows the observer to appreciate the layered construction and hence the airy lightness of the architecture. This impression is further reinforced by the haze effect, which stirs memories of morning mist, and the stadium looking like a spherical "object between heaven and earth."[7] As one of the reference examples in *ARCH+* 131 on the subject of "InFormation. Entfaltung in der Architektur," in which an article by Greg Lynn appears among others, the design not least contributes to the raging debate about digital architecture in the 1990s, which achieved its first visible high point in so-called "blob architecture" (→ Image 26).

75

The Evolution of the Digital Image

Image 21

21

schneider+schumacher

Design for Westhafen Tower, Frankfurt am Main

Analog-digital photomontage
Reproduction of journal image
in: *Bauwelt*, 88, 1997, 31/32 (22 Aug.), p. 1713

1   adm, "Rotierende Quadrate," in *Bauwelt*, 88, 1997, 31/32 (22 Aug.), p. 1713.

2   With thanks to Inga Pothen according to Christian Simons at schneider+schumacher Frankfurt am Main. According to Simons, the image was created by Nicolas Schrabeck.

3   Cf. text → Image 15.

4   Cf. text → Image 16.

A second principal strand by which the digital image makes its entrance into architectural representation practice in addition to the fully digital representation (→ Image 10) is the digital photomontage seen to be increasingly used in the journals from the second half of the 1990s. Whereas the planned new build for the Kop van Zuid former harbor district in Rotterdam was drawn by hand as an illustration in the analog photograph of the project surroundings (→ Image 15), the computer is actually involved in creating this "simulation of the striking tower structure"[1] for the former Westhafen harbor area in Frankfurt some five years later. No perspective drawing or model photography is introduced into the previously taken photograph of the project surroundings. Instead, a rendered design visualization, specifically a digitally generated image element, is used here.

The digital manipulation has so little detrimental effect on the overall photographic impression of the image that it could be confused with a real photograph, at least by the untrained eye. In addition to the knowledge that another version of the design was eventually built, two other aspects are revealing: One, as seen in the earlier examples, is that the glass facade is represented as transparent to allow views into the building's interior and expose the architectural structure. However, the surrounding towers show that the glass should be represented as almost completely mirrorlike in this daylight situation. The second aspect is the lack of a reflection of the new tower in the river. Compared with today's view from the southern end of the Neckar-Main Bridge, whence the photograph of the tower's surroundings was probably taken, the design also looks to have been shifted slightly into the foreground in relation to its surroundings.

The illustration is therefore clearly recognizable as a montage. Nevertheless, it is difficult to decide whether a computer has been involved or not, even for the professional eye. Further research was necessary in this case as well in order to say with certainty that the visualization of the tower involved rendering that was performed in-house with CAD software, specifically MicroStation, which was then inserted into the photograph.[2] It still cannot be said that the montage itself is analog or digital, whether the rendering is photographed or printed out and then glued in, with the image then reproduced in its entirety, or whether it was inserted digitally into the scanned-in photograph of the project's surroundings.

In the journals, the entry of the digital image into representational practice proves to be a hybrid process that takes place in parallel with the fully digital image through the digitalization of the principle of the photomontage, that is to say through the adoption and extension of an established analog process. The rendered model starts to take the place of the photographed model, the imaging process remaining more or less the same.

The illustration is therefore an early example of the second of these "two directions" in the practice of digital architectural images, as had been differentiated in *ARCH+* by 1990:[3] the hybrid analog-digital photomontage in the manner of the materially persuasive simulation,[4] which excels above all through its highly photorealistic component (→ Image 37).

77

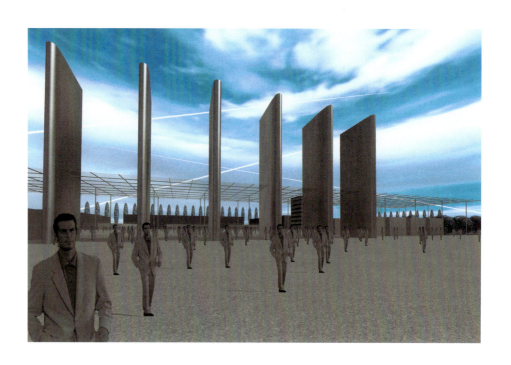

Image 22

22

Matthias Zehle

Schinkel Competition 1997

Rendering
Print of the digital copy
Architectural Museum
of TU Berlin,
Inv. No. SW-A 1997,
02–03

1   Friedhelm Würfel, "Sehen heißt
     verstehen: Architektursimulation
     in der Immobilienmarketing-
     Strategie," in *Immobilien-Zeitung*,
     25.7.1996, No. 16, week 31/32, p. 7.

2   Bus, "'Demokratische'
     Fotofälscher," *taz* dated 15.1.1994
     <https://taz.de/!1581957/>
     (last accessed 26.1.2024).

3   Ibid.

The digitalization of the photomontage is a principal component of hybridization, that is to say the combination and mixing of analog and digital processes and elements, which is first seen in the practice of creating images in the 1990s. This way of working has been given the contemporary name of "mixed media" and is exemplarily outlined by Friedhelm Würfel in 1996 as follows:

"Excellent results can be achieved using computer painting methods. [...] The results of these techniques are always particularly impressive when they are mixed with real photographic material. [...] Of course the methods [...] can be combined with one another: computer models are not only essential for rendering and painting, they are also used very successfully as the basic models in traditional painting and drawing techniques. Model photographs can be digitized and processed on the computer. There are hardly any limits to the various ways of combining these techniques, and the specialist in architectural representation will suggest the most suitable method to the client for each specific case."[1]

Not only rendered designs but also fully digital representations with digitalized photographic image elements are inserted into analog photographs. The unusual reality effects, which can result from this type of digitally inserted and processed image, may give rise to skepticism among the public toward the results of this method of representation. A journal article about an exhibition of renderings at the Bremen City University of Applied Sciences in January 1994 refers to this in a somewhat pointed tone:

"Specialist companies using sophisticated computer programs are able to insert the planned building, which would have previously been drawn only on paper, into real photographs of the future location with such skill that only the trained eye is capable of noticing the counterfeit. To the counterfeiters, no effort is spared in making these images 'photorealistic': They take snaps of real people, parked and driven cars, and ornamental plants to feed into their database."[2]

The journal also states the price, which at that time is "between 15,000 and 20,000 Deutschmarks"[3] for an externally created rendering.

Emerging in the late 1990s, and augmenting the materially persuasive simulation with its aim of representing a design so deceptively real that it looks like photographed reality, is a more relaxed, playful variant of the hybrid architectural image, such as this exemplary visualization from the 1997 Schinkel competition.

This image makes no claim to be either a photorealistic representation or a true-to-reality simulation. With its extremely simplified geometry, reduced range of colors, and contrasting inserted sky, the actual design steps into the background to give a theatrical space for the cloned men in suits. Their repetition takes up the theme of the repetitive character of the design on the one hand, while being an example of the typical digital process of copy and paste, as used here, on the other. Looking rather more surreal than real, this design makes reference to the image form of the collage (→ Image 16), which appears more frequently in the journals for a limited period during the following years (→ Image 25).

The Evolution of the Digital Image

Image 23

23

O&O Baukunst / Franziska
Megert (Visualization)

*Saxon State and University
Library Dresden (SLUB),
Reading Room*

Rendering
Print of the image file
in: *Bauwelt*, 89, 1998,
14 (9 April), p. 761

1   Holger Kleine, "Bücherflimmern
     im Elbsand," in *Bauwelt*, 89,
     1998, 14 (9 April), pp. 758–61,
     here p. 758.

2   Ibid.

3   Ibid., p. 759.

4   Ibid.

5   Cf. <https://www.megert.de/
     com1.html> (last accessed
     26.1.2024).

Even during the second half of the 1990s, when there is a clear increase in the number of renderings appearing in journals compared with the first half of the decade, their numbers in *Bauwelt* continue to be low, at less than an average of thirty per year. Toward the end of the 1990s, the digital image arrives in architectural representation practice, but its use remains the exception rather than a matter of course. Apart from ambitious engineering structures, complex renderings are reserved for well-funded, heavyweight major projects or individual, outstanding prestige buildings.

One such prestige building is the 1995 new build for the Saxon State and University Library Dresden, a cultural building with a high idealistic value beyond technological progressiveness or economic potential. As befitting this excellent reputation, the design is based on a holistic design concept that assumes that "the suggestive qualities of the image worlds made possible by the new media can be absorbed in the built architecture."[1] Under the terms of this design, "the resolution of all surfaces down to the smallest pixel" means that the "facades are resolved into a delicate fabric of irregular stripes, gaps, and shadow lines [...]. Like a picture by the pointillist Seurat, the surfaces positively crumble before the eyes and shimmer,"[2] allowing "the beauty and sensuality of the book to be made into protagonists of the space."[3] This applies to the interior of the building as well. The design envisages that the "shimmering texture of 'real' floor-to-ceiling bookshelves [...] continues uninterrupted into the wood-lined walls of the general reading room and is seen again as a motif on the library tables, the chair upholstery and the floor covering."[4]

As can be seen at first glance, this is also the main aspect intended to be expressed in the visualization of the reading room shown on the opposite page. In accord with the ambitious design, it embodies the early example of a rendering that represents a decidedly artistic design intent. The rendering was created by an external artist, Franziska Megert,[5] who is named in the article as the author. This is not a montage; it is a fully digital representation without any integrated photographic elements (→ Image 10) that already manages to stand out through the half-page, large-format space unusually made available for the visualization in the journal. Here as well, it is less about the deceivingly real, photorealistic representation than the pointed communication of the design concept, achieved in the same way as the "shimmering books," by using mapping that extends over the whole surface. The underside of the ceiling edges makes clear how well the projected texture conceals the simple illumination model and the relatively simple geometry.

The high design quality, including distancing effects such as the almost monochrome color mood, bears witness to the skilled implementation of the compositional methods. The image is therefore an example of a sophisticated rendering showing not only that technological advancement leads to high-quality results but also that it requires an artistic application of the new visualization tools.

81

Image 24

24

Thomas Gräbel,
Heiko Heybey

Schinkel Competition 1998

Analog-digital collage /
montage
Print of the digital copy
Architectural Museum
TU Berlin, Inv. No. SW-A
1998, 01–02

1 Cf. text → Image 22.

In addition to the fully digital representation, the material montage, and the playful collage, the digital image makes its entry into architecture in the time of the hybrid in a multitude of other forms and variants that cannot be clearly assigned to any of the three named types. On the one hand, this casts light on the fact that the assignment made here and the criteria on which it is based are of only a tentative nature. On the other, the phenomenal diversity of architectural images as reflected in the journals can be seen from the threshold of the 1990s right up to the 2000s. The selection presented here contains nowhere near all the forms of appearance of digital architectural images that cannot be fully allocated into the created categories. As Friedhelm Würfel writes in 1996,[1] the "mixed media" method of image creation gives rise to a series of new technical and design possibilities that stem from the combination of analog and digital processes and range between graphic, photo, and rendering, between schematic visualization and photorealistic enhancement, between artistic ambition and the communication of information. The result is a diversity of image forms that do not completely equate with those concepts that are typically associated with analog image design, such as montage or collage.

One example of this is the representation from the 1998 Schinkel competition, which combines and integrates many of these elements. The collage-like nature of the image is expressed here in the montage of the color-rendered design into the black-and-white aerial photograph. The aim here is not to achieve a materially persuasive simulation but rather to emphasize by contrasts not only between the colored design part in the center and the monochrome periphery of the urban context, but also between the detailed texture of the rendering and photograph, possibly faded by the copying process, that forms the underlying location plan. One sign that the computer has been involved is the stretched surface texture of the green loop at the bottom left, but its involvement is evident above all through the copying and pasting of the vegetation, which has not been done using individual items of greenery.

The chosen compositional means give rise to a clear link between the object represented and the type and method of the representation. The graphical intervention on the paper emphasized by the contrasts makes clear the urban planning intervention of the design, which spreads into the existing built environment and assimilates it. The bold and simple color scheme in the manner of an isotherm chart or an altitude contour relief makes reference to a diagram giving extra information about the architectural design.

83

Image 25

25

MVRDV

Flight Forum

Digital collage
Print of the image file
in: *ARCH+*, 1999,
147 (Aug.), p. 65

1   MVRDV, "Flight Forum,"
    in *ARCH+*, 1999, 147 (Aug.),
    pp. 62–65, here p. 65. Due to
    the black-and-white print of the
    journal, this image is also not
    reproduced in color (→ Image 6
    and 10).

2   Bart Lootsma, *Superdutch. Neue
    Niederländische Architektur*,
    Stuttgart and Munich 2000, p. 9.

The boom in journal appearances of the digital collage starts around the end of the 1990s. After the collage underwent digitalization (→ Image 16 and 22) in the course of the 1990s, it creates its own formal style of architectural representation during the time of the practical application of the "mixed media" method at the turn of the millennium. This style can be regarded as typical for this period. In digital photomontages, digital designs are inserted into analog photographs of their surroundings, whereas in digital collages, digitally generated and digitalized photographic image elements are combined to form new digital image spaces using image editing programs such as Photoshop. The analog-digital montage merges into digital-digital montage, as it were. The hybridization of graphical processes continues to advance.

A crucial aspect of this is that digital collages, which are now increasingly incorporated into the journals, disclose their artificially composed character, in contrast to materially persuasive photomontages and to ambitious photorealistic fully digital representations. Rather than hiding their characteristic collage-like style, they elevate it, on the contrary, to a principle of composition. Instead of illusionistic, closed compositions that are intended to suggestively convince observers for a specific purpose, these take, so to speak, an open form. Their objective is not to simulate an actual situation as realistically as possible but to explain an initial concept, an idea or vision, in a playful way.

As the image shows in an exemplary manner, the focus is not so much on adequately visualizing the design but on the associative interpretation of the design context; the actual building remains noticeably undefined, it is only hinted at, vaguely embodied. These types of image are a reduced representation of simplified geometric models without complex illumination or texture, like scenery provided with photographic material to create peculiar landscapes, surreal-real image worlds that stand somewhere between a dream and an abstraction.

This is also the case with this illustration from a series of six images showing the urban concept of a business park near Eindhoven in the Netherlands, which seeks to avoid the waste of valuable usable space and the customary appearance of an industrial area set up on a greenfield site through the rational utilization of the whole site by clustering. Even some selected components of the retained flora and fauna are incorporated into the overall image:

> "A series of 'islands' are left between the asphalt spaghetti and the natural stone business clusters. If each of these islands contains a different type of landscape, this creates a mosaic that also safeguards the ecological integrity of this sensitive fabric. [...] At night, the clusters are illuminated as bright as day, making the business park a 24-hour center of attraction."[1]

The emergence of this open form of digital architectural image is limited in the journals to between the end of the 1990s and the mid-2000s. It is also apparent that, in close association with this observation, the newer architectural consultancies established in the Netherlands in the 1990s are producing "many a sensational design, one after the other."[2] Although this image type is marginal, it is also of interest not least because designers revisit it from around the mid-2010s (→ Image 48) and the digital collage goes through a revival (→ Image 50).

85

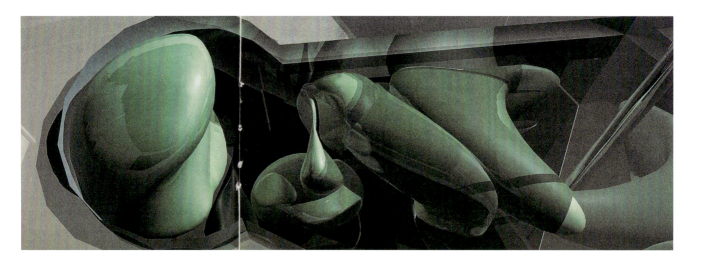

Image 26

26

Greg Lynn

*Installation for the
"Electra '96" Exhibition in
Henie Onstad Kunstsenter
near Oslo*

Rendering
Reproduction of
journal image
in: *Bauwelt*, 91, 2000,
1 (7 Jan.), pp. 26/27

1   Wilhelm Klauser, "Beam me up,
    Scotty," in *Bauwelt*, 91, 2000,
    1 (7 Jan.), pp. 26–27, here p. 26.

2   Cf. Peter Cachola Schmal (ed.),
    *Digital real. Blobmeister, erste
    gebaute Projekte*, exhib. cat.
    DAM Frankfurt, Basel, Boston,
    and Berlin 2001.

3   Klauser, "Beam me up, Scotty,"
    p. 27.

4   Oskar Graf, "Die Statik, die
    Konstruktion und der Dekon-
    struktivismus," in *Bauwelt*, 80,
    1989, 26 (7 July), p. 1260.

5   Florian Böhm, "ACS '95"
    (CAD-Journal 22), in *ARCH+*,
    1995, 129/130 (Dec.), pp. 14–15,
    here p. 15.

6   Greg Lynn, "Das Gefaltete, das
    Biegsame und das Geschmei-
    dige," in *ARCH+*, 1996, 131 (April),
    pp. 62–65, here p. 64.

7   Florian Böhm, "Neue Dimen-
    sionen für die Architektur?,"
    in *ARCH+*, 1999, 148 (Oct.),
    pp. 103–5, here p. 104.

8   Kathy Rae Huffman and
    Margarete Jahrmann, "Elektra
    96," in *Telepolis*, 20.1.1997
    <https://www.telepolis.de/
    features/Elektra-96-3442039.
    html> (last accessed 26.1.2024).

At the beginning of the new millennium, a series of articles appear in the first issue of *Bauwelt* in January 2000 taking the form of an inventory of the status quo under titles such as "The Sliding Shutters," "The Atrium," and "The Disappearance of Simplicity," and describing characteristic aspects of architectural development at the time. The series also includes the article "Beam me up, Scotty" by Wilhelm Klauser, from which the illustration opposite is taken. This article deals with the emergence of a new and strange-looking architectural language of form in the course of the 1990s:

> "One day they were there, and their existence can no longer be argued away. Everyone is in the dark as to which inner state of mind of the architect had seen the benefit of creating the amorphous forms in the first place, what external influences were at play, and why society even gave the necessary acceptance to these forms, leading to their realization at the end of the millennium. No related family trees could be found, and so the new architecture at first appeared astonishingly rootless, and there was something new to visit and admire."[1]

Even though the term is not mentioned here, the description of these "amorphous forms" as "blob" or "blob architecture" was around in the 1990s. It is an ambiguous and controversial term that quickly gained ground to become a cipher and synonym for architecture with the computer, which was thus perceived as such and received programmatically for the first time.[2] Moreover, the article already contains signs of a certain skepticism toward the observed "dissolving of the relationship between construction, geometry, and organic form," and "doubt about the integrity of the proposed solution" arises "in view of the construction costs" for the realization of these complex forms.[3]

It was certainly true with reference to "structures, like those developed by deconstructivists" (→ Image 10) long before the "blob," that these "systems, which are complicated due to their irregularity," could be "analyzed statically as simple, regular systems" with the help of computers—"but at great cost and effort."[4] However, it is now possible in the 1990s "through the 'conversion' of programs [...] used in other fields, such as aeronautical engineering (e.g. IBM CATIA), industrial design or animated cartoon films,"[5] not only to analyze complex constructions (→ Image 20) but also to bring whole buildings "through knotting, twisting, bending, and folding within one form,"[6] even though they must be further processed as "modeled designs in a 3D CAD program with a powerful property specification system."[7] That was not necessary, however, with this illustration. It shows an installation specially designed for "Electra '96," the "first major exhibition of electronic art in Norway."[8]

The Evolution of the Digital Image

Image 27

27

Nietz, Prasch, Sigl,
Tchoban, Voss /
Picture Factory Schmidt +
Würfel GbR (Visualization)

*Major Project
"DomAquarée" Berlin*

Rendering
Print of the image file
in: *Bauwelt*, 92, 2001,
17 (4 May), p. 18

1   For example, the *ARCH+* "CAD
     Journal" ends after its last issue
     120/130/1995.

2   See *Computer Spezial. Software
     für Architekten, Ingenieure und
     Bauunternehmen*, 2001, 3, pp. 2,
     18–19.

3   Jens Guthoff, "Architekturgrafik
     mit CAD" (*ARCH+*-Baumarkt), in
     ARCH+, 1990, 102 (Jan.), p. 89.

4   Friedhelm Würfel, "Sehen heißt
     verstehen: Architektursimulation
     in der Immobilienmarketing-
     Strategie," in *Immobilien-Zeitung*,
     25.7.1996, No. 16, week 31/32, p. 7.
     Cf. text → Image 41.

Even when the critical analysis of computer graphics as a new technical medium of design visualization clearly subsides from the mid-1990s in the journals,[1] the hype about rendering is not yet at an end. The digital image as a novelty merely receded from the focus of media attention. In fact, the number of image appearances in *Bauwelt* steps up sharply from the start of the 2000s, and doubles in 2001 compared with the figure for 1997 to reach its highest-ever level. Rendering has now established itself alongside model photography in the journals and continues to spread at an increasing rate. The boom in the digital image is starting. In the same year, for example, the Bertelsmann supplement *Computer Spezial*, which was first published in 1986, introduces a new section specifically about "Visualization."[2]

This design visualization is from an issue of *Bauwelt* in the same year. It is among the first journal illustrations to assert a claim to be photorealistic, which is also evident from its appearance. The aim here is not so much the artistic, didactic, playful, or schematic communication of the fundamental idea behind the design as it is to achieve the greatest possible realism in the representation of a fictional scene as if it were previously photographed reality. It does not start from a photograph into which the digitally created design is inserted but rather the other way round. Colors, textures, illumination, and light effects are applied to a 3D computer model to which staffage in the form of photographic elements is added to achieve a realistic-looking everyday scene. Created in the digital space by image editing programs, the image is a mixture of a fully digital representation and a photomontage.

That it was created using a montage-like process is still apparent. The inserted people are certainly positioned very carefully and precisely integrated into the context by shadows and reflections, as shown, for example, by the shadows of the feet of the striding man in the right-hand corner of the image. On closer inspection, however, the figures and objects look as if they are cutouts. The photographic material of the staffage combines with the rendered design but does not form a homogeneous, coherent image effect. This is successfully compensated for by the well-designed illumination effects. The strong, inclined shadows of the roof ribs overlay the facade grid and fall like a net over the whole scene to act as a connecting element, with the ribs also reflecting in the glass balcony panels and the right-hand facade. The highly realistic effect stems therefore from the staged lighting situation, with the strong, inclined shadows of the repeating elements generally playing an important part in achieving this degree of photorealism.

The image makes clear in an exemplary manner the further development of the first of the "two directions" spoken of earlier in *ARCH+* in 1990: "so-called photorealistic representations, […] which the layperson cannot distinguish from photographs."[3] (→ Image 32 and 41) The main purpose for the use of this compositional means is to show what the finished state of the building would look like from the viewpoint of the potential users. This type of pictorial staging of the planned arcade architecture as a sunny, pulsating urban place is intended to appeal to them as part of a visual communication "in which a sender can create a specific idea in the mind of the receiver via a medium."[4]

89

Image 28

28

Benedict Tonon

*Project Multiplex Theater
Berlin City West, Foyer*

(Team member in
the competition:
Rochus Wiedemer)
Rendering
Reproduction
of journal image
in: *Bauwelt*, 93, 2002,
43/44 (22 Nov.), p. 17

1   Cf. Winfried Nerdinger (ed.),
     *Die Architekturzeichnung.
     Vom barocken Idealplan zur
     Axonometrie*, Munich 1986.

2   *Bauwelt*, 87, 1996, 25 (5 July),
     p. 1474.

3   Ibid., p. 1478.

4   *Bauwelt*, 87, 1996, 48 (27 Dec.),
     pp. 2692–93.

5   *Bauwelt*, 89, 1998, 12 (27 Mar.),
     p. 568.

6   Ibid.

7   *Bauwelt*, 90, 1999, 6 (5 Feb.),
     p. 260.

8   *Bauwelt*, 93, 2002, 46 (6 Dec.),
     p. 29.

9   *domus*, 2000, 884 (Nov.), p. 50.

In contrast to the digital design visualizations based on the photographic approach, this image apparently seeks to deliberately dispense with the characteristic features of photorealistic representation. Here as well, a computer-created 3D geometric model forms the basis and the starting point for the visualization. However, this visualization relies neither on complex texturing of the surfaces nor on lighting effects, and certainly not on an illumination model. Instead, the compositional means are reduced, on the one hand, to the simple line drawing of the CAD model and, on the other, the uniform coloration of the surfaces in beige combined with a lighter and a darker gray.

With this ascetic use of the digital representation means, however, the visualization is less about a decisive rejection of digital photorealism, which is beginning to spread in the architectural journals. The illustration much more represents a late example of a specific feature of the digital image in practical architectural representation, which can be traced back in the journals to the early 1990s and is seen rather more as a self-contained practical approach to digital image design, an alternative to the complex and cost-intensive renderings in the early phase of computer graphics (→ Image 14).

Instead of getting involved with creating the most photorealistic imitation of reality—which is actually not possible at this time in any case, given the available technical resources, even with a great deal of expense and effort—the compositional approach focuses on the architecture. It achieves the effect by adopting the tradition of color-washed or colored architectural drawings[1] and consciously reduces its graphical means to outlines and color.

The numbers of this kind of representation may be too small for it to be spoken of as a type or even a style. However, this image is not an isolated example; it is one manifestation of a significant phenomenon that appears in the journals for about ten years, from the beginning of the 1990s to the beginning of the 2000s. The first to be seen there are designs by Hans Kollhoff, followed by others such as Max Dudler,[2] Ortner & Ortner,[3] Dieter Hoffmann-Axthelm and Bernd Albers,[4] Walter A. Noebel,[5] Rave Architekten,[6] Kahlfeldt Architekten,[7] and Hansjörg Göritz + Werkgefährten.[8] The approach is found elsewhere, for example in Oswald Mathias Ungers's contribution to the Pergamon Museum in Berlin.[9] This phenomenon then disappears again from the journals.

91

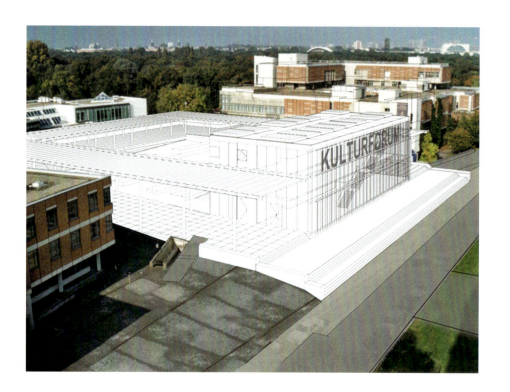

Image 29

29

Katja Kühn

Schinkel Competition 2002

Analog-digital
photomontage
Print of the digital copy
Architectural Museum
TU Berlin, Inv. No. SW-A
2002, 02–04

1   Cf. Peter Wels, *Architektur-zeichnungen*, with a foreword by Manfred Sack, Hamburg 1993.

2   For example, Helge Bofinger (ed.), *Helmut Jacoby—Meister der Architekturzeichnung*, exhib. cat. DAM Frankfurt, Tübingen and Berlin 2001; Hans Schätzke (ed.), *Die Hand des Architekten. Zeichnungen aus Berliner Architektursammlungen*, Cologne 2002; Gustav Peichl, *Back to the pen—back to the pencil*, Salzburg and Munich 2003; Anja Hartmann (ed.), *Handgezeichnete Visionen. Eine Sammlung aus deutschen Architekturbüros*, Berlin 2004.

3   Tchoban Foundation (ed.), *Museum für Architekturzeich-nung. Museum for Architectural Drawing*, Berlin [2017].

4   For example, the conference "The End of Architectural Drawings?," Rome, November 2018 <https://arthist.net/archive/19279> (last accessed 27.1.2024).

5   Cf. text → Image 15 and 16.

While the digital image may also appear in the 1990s in the form of the traditional architectural drawing (→ Image 28), hand-drawn design representations are appearing noticeably less often in the journals at the end of the 1990s and have as good as disappeared by the beginning of the 2000s. One of the last architectural drawings is found in issue 48/2003 of *Bauwelt* and comes from Peter Wels, one of the widely known specialist architectural draftsmen in Germany.[1] This process takes place gradually in the journals and largely without attracting much attention, while a new public and journalistic interest in the architectural drawing is observed at the same time.[2] Over time, this interest manifests also on an institutional level,[3] which has continued up to the present day[4]—an indication of the sustained explosiveness and virulence of the fundamental change in media from analog to digital images in architecture. From the beginning of the 2010s, therefore, architectural drawings are again to be found in the journals (→ Image 48).

On the other hand, this image represents a further step in the process of hybridization of analog representation methods, namely the digitalization of drawing on a photograph as a form of photomontage.[5] At first glance, it is recognized as a montage. The design is not rendered but was created as a simple line drawing with a CAD program and then positioned in an analog photograph of the project surroundings using image processing software. What shows it to be a computer drawing and not a hand-drawn perspective is that, in some parts of the drawing, the lines of the drawing include the volumes of the surrounding buildings, which immediately draws the eye to the discrepancy between the perspective of the design and that of the photograph—a situation that a hand drawing would surely have eliminated. After a longer inspection, the transparently overpainted cars under the gray road surfacing stand out in the bottom right of the image, which points to the situation in the street in the original photograph being different from the one depicted. In the same way, the gray of the dead-end street over the green lawn points to post-editing of a digital image.

Overall, these details lead to the assumption that graphical methods have been used in an attempt to adjust the perspective of the photo to that of the design with the aim of concealing their disagreement. However, when the pronounced curvature of the horizon is taken into account, it seems more likely that the discrepancy in the perspectives is due to the distortion of the wide-angle lens used. Regarded in this light, it would have been necessary to curve the representation of the design in order to match it to the perspective of the photograph.

Taking everything into consideration, this is a special form of photomontage that combines the open character of a drawing with the realism of a photograph. The representation is not intended to make the design appear deceptively real, using true photographs, but rather to openly reveal its montage character and, what's more, deliberately emphasize that fact. The status of the design as something possible, something provisional, instead of something allegedly already existing is preserved by this approach.

93

Image 30

30

Mark Braun

SAP Office Building Berlin

Rendering
Reproduction of
journal image
in: *Bauwelt*, 94, 2003,
8 (21 Feb.), p. 16

1   In the private papers of Mark
    Braun (1962–2008) at the
    Architectural Archives at the
    Academy of Arts, Archive and
    Library, Berlin, no data file of
    the image had been retained.
    According to information kindly
    supplied by Karenine Reber, it
    was created by Olaf Bünck.

2   The first blue hour representation
    is found in *Bauwelt*, 92, 2001,
    17 (4 May), p. 15.

The start of the 2000s is accompanied not only by a clear rise in the number of digital images recorded in the journals but also by an increase in the quality of renderings with respect to the representation of illumination and light effects. Images emerge that, in addition to depicting the design as a highly photorealistic and materially persuasive simulation, are also intended to endow the representation with a specific mood and thus lend it a certain atmosphere.

Here is an early example of such a representation. It is a rendered design of a proposed office building that is inserted into the photo of its future location so that it looks as if it already exists. Clearly visible is the halftone dot pattern of the journal, which is due to the original's small image format being only 8.5 × 5 cm.[1] In comparison with the light-flooded arcade architecture in *Bauwelt* 17/2001 (→ Image 27), the design is not staged here in a daylight simulation of the project in typical use, but rather in a particular light mood: in the moment of evening twilight, known as the blue hour, a traditional topos often poetically taken up in art and literature, film, and photography.

The mood of the image is not determined by the contrast of light and shadow but by a synthesizing effect that arises from the chosen light mood at the threshold of day turning into night, with its flowing transition from the warm blue of the sky to the turquoise of the illuminated building, yellow and red lights of the traffic, and the violet of the sidewalk. This light mood awakens typical urban associations, while the individual image elements combine to create a coherent image effect. The twilight of the blue hour above all allows the simultaneous depiction of the design's surroundings and its interior. The image presents the building as an urban body of light, while allowing its special architectural features to be displayed, such as the glass facade horizontally divided by the intermediate floor slabs and roof. A black night sky would have made the integration of the building into the urban context disappear in the darkness. A realistic representation in daylight would have turned the transparent glass facade into its opposite, a reflective dark mass.

Even though the visualization of light and illumination is very advanced for its time in this image, the facades in the representation still lack the reflections of the light sources outside the building. Streetlights, the lights of the traffic, the silhouettes of the neighboring buildings, the residual daylight in the dusk sky are not overlain as reflections on the glass in the depiction of the view into the building through the facade. This clearly indicates that the image is a rendering and not a photograph. The people, too, are obviously inserted into the image. In contrast to the long exposure lines from the car lights, the people are shown as static and free of any blurring due to movement.

As one of the first examples of a depiction of the blue hour light mood,[2] which later becomes firmly established and further developed in digital architectural image practice in the journals as a mode of representation (→ Image 34 and 47), this image shows the qualitative advances in the rendering technique from the 2000s in the direction of a closed, illusionistic image capable of creating a specific atmosphere.

The Evolution of the Digital Image

Image 31

Anne Niemann,
Johannes Ingrisch

Landmark East Dunwich

Rendering
Print of the image file
in: *Bauwelt*, 95, 2004,
18 (7 May), p. 18

1   fr, "Landmark East," in *Bauwelt*,
    95, 2004, 18 (7 May), p. 18. All
    other quotations: ibid.

2   Cf. text → Image 47.

This illustration, which really represents something new, an absolute innovation in its genre, at least in the context of *Bauwelt* and *ARCH+*, shows how atmospheres can also be created with simple compositional methods. The crucial factor allowing this may be said with certainty to have been the special design context. It is the visualization from a competition for a landmark, which is intended to be an economy-boosting "identification object for the region" in eastern England.[1] The design therefore does not refer to architecture in the narrower sense; it "foresees the six churches in the town of Dunwich that had largely sunk into the sea over time, as redesigned steel sculptures." By siting them in their authentic locations, which are now under the sea, they would "establish the coast and the uncontrollable forces of nature that continually change the course of shorelines and rivers as a symbol of the East of England." The design concept is based on a historical silhouette assisted by some architectural staging, which seems to float above the sea, and with its outline forms symbolically refers to memories of the lost place beyond the coastline of today.

This unusual combination of monument, art installation, and tourist attraction offers a legitimate opportunity to distance this image from visualizations based on ordinary representational practice. The sacred monumentality of the sea is captured as a sublime, never-ending natural space and combined with the secretive mystique of a submerged place from the Middle Ages into a dramatic staging from which a solemn calm and enthralling stillness flow. This impressive effect is based on the use of simple but effective methods. In fact, it uses digitalized and edited images of English church architecture, which are inserted into a photograph of the sea, which cannot be said for certain to have been taken at Dunwich or some other coastal location.

The crucial point is the subsequent coloring of the complete photograph, the artificial reduction of its natural spectrum of color to a monochrome bottle or sea green, which also shines through the transparently represented buildings. Thus the radiating sunlight of the daylight photograph suggests the impression of shimmering moonlight breaking through the clouds and falling on the submerged churches to make them appear even more mystical.

This anticipates the compositional means for achieving a homogeneous image effect that will later be used again and again in digital architectural representation practice in journals. It is a simple trick used to great effect, be it through actual monochrome, through desaturation, or by reducing the color palette to a specific spectrum (→ Image 39, 44, and 45). The homogeneous effect is based on minimizing the natural phenomenal diversity and following that up with a reduction in the number of represented details, which are often revealing and, in many cases, prevent a realistic image impression from being created. It is not unusual for a few features that have been over-detailed or not carefully enough depicted—mainly in the field of staffage—to put off the observer and frustrate attempts to achieve a synthetic overall effect.[2]

97

The Evolution of the Digital Image

Image 32

32

Christoph Mäckler
Architekten

*Competition Terminal 3
Frankfurt am Main
Airport (2005),
Interior Perspective*[1]

Rendering
Print of the image file
in: *Bauwelt*, 96, 2005,
25 (1 July), p. 18

1   With kind thanks to Fraport AG
     for approval to use the image.

2   See for example the visualizations
     of the reconstruction of Braun-
     schweig Schloss in *Bauwelt*, 95,
     2004, 1/2 (9 Jan.) or the European
     Central Bank (EZB) building in
     Bauwelt, 2004, 13 (2 April). Cf.
     text → Image 23.

In the first half of the 2000s, renderings of various qualities appear in *Bauwelt*. They are normally seen in small image format, which is needed to fit into the layout of the competition parts of the journal. Large-format computer visualizations are the exception and are mostly found in certain special issues of the journals, for example issue 13/2003 about the German competition for Olympia 2012 and issue 40/41 in 2004 for the reconstruction of the old Milan trade fair center. As a rule, they take the form of complex presentation images produced by larger architectural practices for suitable major projects or eminent clients.[2]

Another such instance is found in *Bauwelt* issue 25/2005 "Terminal 3" about the architectural competition held by Fraport AG for the building of a third terminal to expand Frankfurt airport, anticipating the closure of the Rhine-Main Air Base operated by the US Air Force since 1945, which duly closed at the end of 2005. The issue contains a whole series of large-format visualizations that take up half a page of the journal each, with some of the illustrations measuring 21 × 15 cm.

The photorealistic claims of the fully digital representation, with the inserted staffage of photographic image elements, are plain to see. The rendered representation of the interior perspective of the planned terminal hall fills all the image space. The carefully positioned people are meant to suggest a typical situation occurring every day at the airport. Great emphasis is placed on the reproduction of the materiality of the natural stone floor tiles, which reflect the architecture and staffage in their polished surface. Apart from the taxis stopping in front of the terminal building, sky and clouds make up almost all the abstract view out. The representation is neither schematic nor didactic. The compositional means are used in such a way that an extremely realistic impression is created.

It must be said, however, that the eye is drawn and distracted by the inconsistent reflections of architecture and staffage. Compressed reflections, such as those of the fashionably dressed woman and the two pilots, would occur only if the floor of the hall were steeply sloping.

Instead of creating a light-flooded or atmospheric effect (→ Image 27 and 30), the representation expresses a material, businesslike style. An austere, serious tone prevails, which makes the image no less of a carefully considered and arranged pictorial staging of the architectural design, the object of which is to highlight the grand scale, simplicity, and spaciousness of the terminal hall. In order to publish the image and comply with today's relevant legislation, the faces of some of the mounted people had to be blurred by subsequently applying a soft-focus lens tool due to stricter data protection laws.

99

The Evolution of the Digital Image

Image 33

33

Christian Kollmer

Schinkel Competition 2005

Rendering
Print of the digital copy
Architectural Museum
TU Berlin, Inv. No. SW-A
2005, 01–04

1   *Bauwelt*, 91, 2000, 29 (4 Aug.),
     p. 19 top right; *ARCH+*, 2001,
     154/155 (Jan.), pp. 78/79;
     Bauwelt, 93, 2002, 3 (18 Jan.),
     p. 38 top; *Bauwelt*, 93, 2002,
     46 (6 Dec.), p. 27; ibid., p. 28 left.

2   Friederike Meyer in conversation
     with Christoph Reichen and
     Malte Kloes from bildbau, in
     Bauwelt, 107, 2016, 33 (26 Aug.),
     pp. 26–29, here p. 28.

3   Cf. text → Image 17.

Before the first blue hour representations (→ Image 30), another compositional feature appears in the journals. This newcomer characterizes the digital architectural image in the 2000s: the use of light and illumination effects such as glare and overexposure in combination with soft focus and transparency effects to suggest strongly sunlit, gleaming white, lively and milky blurred, light-flooded image spaces that, together with their staffage, appear to dissolve in light. Everything is airy, light, and bright. People and objects look translucent, see-through, almost ghost-like, or disappear in the extreme blurriness of their movements.

This compositional phenomenon also has its own boom time in the journals. The first representation with a glaring white flare effect appears in 2000 in *Bauwelt*, the first gleaming white scene one year later in *ARCH+*, the first transparent staffage elements appear in 2002 in *Bauwelt*, the first light-flooded and the first milky, blurred three-dimensionalities are seen in the same journal.[1] The heyday of this glaring white, blurred, transparent style comes in the second half of the 2000s. Its use decreased sharply after this (→ Image 40) and was succeeded by golden, warm light (→ Image 34 and 41) and dramatic, romantic light moods of every description (→ Image 43, 45, and 49).

One possible explanation for this decline is offered by the interview with Malte Kloes and Christoph Reichen from the visualization agency bildbau GmbH in *Bauwelt* 33/2016 in which the two professional architectural image designers take a look back over their own practices:

"[MK] At the beginning, we often worked with, for example, pre-configured filters such as 'glamour-glow.' They are filters which blur the white areas in the image and quickly create a mood. Over time, however, we noticed that these quickly created effects often distracted from what was important. [...] [CR] Such filters often suppress the detail and banalize the image. They wipe out everything the architect and visualizer have spent a lot of time seeking to achieve."[2]

On the other hand, this illustration, an early example taken from the 2005 Schinkel competition, shows the deliberate use of these light effects to amplify the intended image statement. It contains neither blurred people nor objects, nor is the room flooded with glaring sunlight. The outdoor space appears to be filled with a thick mist, allowing the glass facade to reflect the interior space, which, with its overexposed white stools, sunlit columns, and generally excessively white image elements, is shown to its best advantage. Appearing for the first time here is also the clearly discernible effect of indirect, diffuse light propagation, through which the underside of the gallery, in the back part of the room and above the bar, reflects the color of the wooden parquet and changes from yellow to violet and then darkens as it approaches the walls. Light can now be represented as considerably more complex and relational instead of just as a global parameter.

Last but not least, this image is also an example of how computer hardware and suitable design and visualization programs have become so affordable that students and smaller architectural practices can use them and thus create photorealistic renderings like those of established, major firms of architects.[3]

The Evolution of the Digital Image

Image 34

34

BEHF Architekten

*Department Store
Tyrol Innsbruck*

Rendering
Print of the image file
in: *Bauwelt*, 97, 2006,
47 (8 Dec.), p. 12

1   Felix Zwoch, "Brauchte die
    Bauwelt ein Re-Design? Muss
    sie mit dem Zeitgeist Schritt
    halten?," in *Bauwelt*, 97, 2006,
    37 (1 Oct.), p. 2.

2   Cf. text → Image 32.

3   Cf. text → Image 16.

In 2006, the number of renderings appearing in *Bauwelt* doubles in comparison with the figure for 2000. In the same year, *Bauwelt* undertakes a "redesign," in terms of both its content and its graphics, which affects its own image reproduction practice, in issue 37 in October. The introduction states: "The layout is more stringent, the images are arranged in blocks and tell their own story in addition to that in the text and are set apart from the text by white islands."[1] As a glance into the competition part of the journal shows, the most noticeable aspect is that the images are also larger and more numerous. Half-page illustrations in combination with smaller formats are no longer the exception but have now become the rule.[2] More space has been granted for the digital image. As the example of the "redesign" of *Bauwelt* in 2006 clearly demonstrates, the emergence of the digital architectural image in the journals is also due to editorial decisions.

The aesthetic development of the digital architectural image at the start of the 2000s is strongly shaped by technological development. A more pronounced shift toward compositional variation and stylistic differentiation is being spoken about from around the middle of the same decade. It must be stressed that these statements do not apply to the avant-garde of the technically possible but rather to general trends in digital architectural image practice as discerned in the printed medium of the journal.

Thus the large-format representation of a lighting situation showing the twilight of the blue hour (→ Image 30) makes way for a golden light mood for the first time at the end of 2006 in the competition part of issue 47. Crucial to the image effect here is no longer the cool, blue-note ambiance at the threshold of day and night but the delicate pink of the onset of the evening red sky and the warm yellow light of artificial lighting, which together create a celebratory atmosphere—a kind of restrained glow that spreads out as a golden, warm shimmer over the whole image and melds it into a single aesthetic whole.

In this case, the image is also a photomontage, in which the rendered design is inserted into a photograph of the project's surroundings and then digitally edited. Although the rendered part is easy to recognize as such, it is not as easy to find at first glance. On the one hand, the proposed building takes up the pastel colors of the evening light reflected in its own windows and the interior light emitted through them, in the same way as those of the neighboring photographed buildings, to create the light mood in the photograph. On the other hand, the photograph itself is designed to give the observers the perspective of the people strolling down the street for an evening walk around town, and to direct their eyes initially past the design and along the slight curve of the street onto the mountain panorama in the background. Therefore, it is only on a second, more attentive look that the strollers are revealed to have been subsequently introduced into the photograph.

Overall, the image imparts a sense of festiveness, which the represented scene endeavors to elevate over and above its everyday banality. The future built reality is not intended to be represented only photorealistically. The aim is much more to add further aesthetic value beyond the actual architectural object by creating a specific atmosphere, a certain mood using compositional means. The materially persuasive simulation (→ Image 32) becomes an emotionally persuasive simulation.[3]

103

The Evolution of the Digital Image

Image 35

35

Entasis Arkitekter

*Former Carlsberg Brewery
Site Copenhagen*

Rendering
Print of the image file
in: *Bauwelt*, 98, 2007,
24 (22 June), p. 9

1 Cf. text → Image 51.

2 See e.g. the car positioned to
clarify the scale in → Image 9.

3 Jan Geipel, "Carlsberg-Areal in
Kopenhagen," in *Bauwelt*, 98,
2007, 24 (22 June), pp. 8–10,
here p. 9.

During the year after the "redesign," the number of digital images appearing in *Bauwelt* reaches its then-current high point and the second-highest total of the observed period between 1980 and 2020, which will not be exceeded until 2018.[1] The journal, so it would appear, is reacting to a practice that is already quite commonplace in architectural design. The numbers of model photographs diminish accordingly. They do not disappear completely from the journals, but they finally cease to be the prevalent image medium for representing designs. Drawings are no longer to be seen in journals. By the mid-2000s, the digital visualization boom in architecture is fully underway. The age of the large digital presentation image begins.

With that appears a further feature of digital composition that certainly does not represent a genuine digital innovation. However, with advancing spread and design differentiation of the digital architectural image, it is increasingly found in journals and can be legitimately described as a narrative moment.

Irrespective of whether a design representation is specifically meant to emotionalize its subject or to reproduce it as accurately as possible, the representation is always a staging, by intention or not, be it rendered, photographed, or drawn. In its representation, the imagined building is necessarily placed by pictorial means in the scene, whether lifelike or abstract, whether suggestive or didactic, photorealistic or surreal, with or without staffage, in daylight or twilight. To this extent, a picture always tells a story: the scene that it depicts, which may go more or less unnoticed[2] or which may be deliberately brought to the fore.

In this illustration, the narrative moment is made explicit for the first time, in an almost poster-art style, as the central compositional element of the representation. The design is from an entry for an architectural competition to come up with ideas for the future use of a site formerly occupied by a Danish brewing firm as an "urban quarter for work, leisure, and education," and shows people able to "jump directly from the brewery into the pool."[3] The design visualization captures this moment precisely. A young man stands high above the swimming pool on a springboard and is obviously being encouraged by the people in the water to overcome his fears and risk the jump. His indecision is emphasized by his posture, half-turned to the observer. Only his head is turned toward the pool. The design itself is shown in a relatively simplified style. The planned glazing clearly shows reflections. In this illustration, the mood is set by the complementary contrast of the brick red of the buildings and the blue-green water. An abstract background has been chosen for the representation.

As demonstrated quite pertinently here, the narrative moment can tell a story by visual means in which the actual architectural design is embedded as in a plot. The presented scene provides both the access and the vehicle for considering the architecture, giving the design semantic added value by the type and manner of its pictorial staging (→ Image 37 and 42).

Image 36

36

Herzog & de Meuron

Theater and Concert Center Hamburg

Rendering
Print of the image file
in: *Bauwelt*, 99, 2008,
1/2 (4 Jan.), p. 55

1   jomi, "Philharmonie auf dem Kaispeicher?," *Hamburger Abendblatt* dated 27.6.2003, p. 11.

2   Andreas Quart, "Philharmonie Hamburg," in *Bauwelt*, 94, 2003, 27/28 (25 July), p. 2.

3   Hubertus Adam, "Nutzungs-mischung Philharmonie," in *Bauwelt*, 99, 2008, 1/2 (4 Jan.), pp. 52–55, here p. 52.

4   Ibid., p. 54.

5   Ibid., p. 52.

6   Ibid., p. 54.

7   See Alex Schröder, "Wie Hamburg die Notbremse zog," DLF Kultur, 1.2.2018 <https://www.deutschlandfunkkultur.de/kostenexplosion-bei-der-elbphilharmonie-wie-hamburg-die-100.html> (last accessed 28.1.2024).

8   The image was created by Christian Zöllner as an employee of HdeM. With thanks to Christian Zöllner. The first renderings are published in the *Hamburger Abendblatt*.

9   Hubert Locher, "Mythogene Fotografie—Architektur, Fotografie, Gemeinschaft," in *Architektur Fotografie. Darstellung—Verwendung—Gestaltung*, ed. Hubert Locher and Rolf Sachsse, Berlin and Munich 2016, pp. 178–203, here p. 183.

10 *Ultimative Reiseziele Deutschland. Die Top-250-Liste von Lonely Planet*, Ostfildern 2021, pp. 18–19.

More than almost any other example, the well-known case of the Elbphilharmonie theater and concert center in Hamburg manages to illustrate the impact that the digital architectural image can have. The building of a glazed concert hall on the former quayside storage warehouse Kaispeicher A in the Hamburg harbor district was recognized from the beginning as a "'unique opportunity to create an architectural icon'"[1] that, with its symbolic form of a jagged wave, would be "the makings [...] of an internationally recognized landmark of Hamburg,"[2] and it was not least a "handful of visualizations"[3] that contributed to "reality [...] emerging from an idée fixe."[4] Arising out of the first public presentation of the project in summer 2003, "the idea had matured through the suggestive renderings of Herzog & de Meuron into a form that triggered an unprecedented enthusiasm at the level of political decision-makers as well as among the general public [...] the image presented by Herzog & de Meuron was so powerful that its realization was able to start [...] as little as four years later."[5]

Even later, when the project was threatened with failure due to rising costs, it was again digital images of the future building that ensured the public's interest did not wane and contributed to a spending wave "that was exceeded only by that for the reconstruction of the Dresden Frauenkirche";[6] at that time, however, the total cost of 800 million euros, the ultimate price tag upon completion of the building in 2016, was not foreseen.[7] The image opposite is a rendering from 2007 of the planned complex, comprising the philharmonic hall, luxury apartments, hotel, restaurants, bars, and a panoramic public plaza, atmospherically shining out as the city's nocturnal illuminated city crown set in the hazy surroundings of Hamburg harbor.[8] In a literal sense, the atmosphere (from the Greek *atmos*: vapor) of the drizzly weather is almost physically perceptible. At the same time, the diffuse nocturnal light allows the use of a reduced color scheme, which benefits the homogeneous impression of the image. Consequently, a first glance fails to notice that the reflections of light in the water at the bottom of the quay wall obviously come from the photograph of the original situation, into which the design has been inserted.

The digital image stages the future building as an exposed urban monument radiating its own aura like a mythogenic photograph "elaborating the symbolic potential of the building in a directly evident way as its connotation, allowing observers to experience it and therefore invest it with value."[9] Unlike the photograph, the digital visualization anticipates the identity-promoting quality of the constructed building while it is still in the unphotographable design state. In 2021, the "Elphie" claimed third place in the *Lonely Planet* Top 250 list for Germany, just behind Leipzig and Lake Constance.[10]

107

Image 37

37

Gramazio & Kohler

New Synagogue Potsdam

Rendering
Print of the image file
in: *Bauwelt*, 100, 2009,
19 (15 May), p. 11

1   Cf. text → Image 35.

2   Cf. text → Image 42.

This illustration is a further example of the continuing influence of the photomontage principle in the practice of digital architectural representation (→ Image 21). At the same time, it is also an example showing that there is only a gradual difference between material and emotionalizing representations, and the transition between the two modes can be fluid.

A photograph taken of the site before any development took place is also used here as the basis for the final image into which the design is digitally inserted and then edited. Here the photographic part is so large, and the manipulation done so discreetly, that the image could be mistaken for a photograph, at least by the untrained eye. In addition to the desaturated, slightly overexposed left-hand half of the image, the main giveaway is the people on the sidewalk, some of whom appear to be floating and are obviously taken from different illumination contexts. To these telltale features can be added the facade of the Potsdam City Palace at the end of the street: rebuilding was due to commence in the next year and so a historical photograph was pragmatically cut to size and pasted in.

The design itself is integrated so subtly into the image that it appears to be part of the photograph. Aside from the connection to the building in the foreground, the detailed reflections in the windows, and the continuous shadow on the facade, this convincing effect is mainly due to the photograph. Neither the special moment of the blue hour, the still-cheerful evening sunshine, nor the artificial lighting (→ Image 30, 34, and 36) are crucial here; it is the natural lighting mood similar to that of the morning hours of a cold, clear winter day captured at the location with the camera. Half-bathed in the even, mildly intensive light of this particular season and time of day, half-decked in shadow, the color palette consists of only a few pastel shades: blue, yellow, orange, and red. To this can be added the gray of the cobblestone road surface and the dark brown of the bare trees. Gaudy or pure colors play no part; likewise there is very little green. This specific light and color regime creates a unifying, homogenizing effect in which the design, with its amber-colored travertine facade, integrates so harmoniously into the image that the observer almost overlooks the merely schematically depicted neighboring building to the right of the design.

Photograph and rendering merge in a discreet way to form an aesthetic whole, without contributing any aesthetic added value by way of further efforts to optimize the staging. Even if the image effect here is due more to the realistic impression of the photograph than the compositional reworking, this photomontage does not represent a materially faithful simulation. The effect comes much more out of a mood stemming from the narrative potential,[1] which is already inherent in the photograph:[2] the real atmosphere of a bright, clear winter morning as a scenic setting for the fictional gathering of the congregation in front of their new meeting house.

109

The Evolution of the Digital Image

Image 38

38

Wulf Böer,
Simon Lindhuber

Schinkel Competition 2009

Rendering
Print of the digital copy
Architectural Museum
TU Berlin, Inv. No. SW-A
2009, 01-01

1   Cf. text → Image 25.

2   *Bauwelt*, 99, 2008, 26 (11 July),
    p. 13; *Bauwelt*, 100, 2009,
    17/18 (8 May), p. 12; *Bauwelt*,
    100, 2009, 27/28 (24 July), p. 47;
    Bauwelt, 101, 2010, 15 (16 April),
    p. 10.

3   Cf. e.g. Alfred Kastl, *Filter,
    Vorsatzlinsen, Weichzeichner*
    (Wiphota Series, 10), Unterschon-
    dorf 1953.

Even toward the end of the 2000s, a few examples of digital design representations not based on collages, as were popular in the years around the turn of the millennium,[1] but in a certain way comparable to them appear in the journals and in the image material for the Schinkel competition. These representations depart from the closed form of the photorealistic image as well, instead presenting the subject in a somewhat more open form; in other words, they allow the subject to show its image character instead of illusively concealing it (→ Image 29).

The composition is often based on the example of a physical architectural model, which allows a simplified, schematic representation to communicate the intended statement by genuine architectural means. While the digital image in its early phase could appear somewhat unintentionally like a model (→ Image 14), the digitally simulated model can now be differentiated through its composition, perhaps by partial coloring, by referring to the insert model, or as a virtual or digitally post-processed model photograph.[2]

If photorealistic rendering normally means the representation of materiality in terms of texture and color and the realistic-appearing reproduction of natural or artificial light, then this illustration to a certain extent embodies a type of photorealistic representation, even if its focus is on neither materiality nor light. It adopts an optical effect that stems from the field of photography—like, for example, the soft-focus lens[3]—and uses it to represent a specific photographic phenomenon. As can be seen in the image, only the residential complex in the foreground is reproduced in sharp focus, while the context in the background is blurred. This strong contrast in the sharpness of the image, also known as the tilt-shift effect, is intended to simulate a macro photograph of a miniature landscape and lend the representation the specific character of a model.

Like many other compositional means, such as working with color and black-and-white monochrome or alternating detail and abstraction (→ Image 24 and 39), this playing with the image definition can also be used to create the observer's view of the image. The aim is to focus on specific aspects of the represented design and emphasize them as being important, while attenuating less important aspects and shifting them away from the center of attention.

That is the case here, where, with the help of image definition and the bird's-eye perspective, the animated roof landscape is moved into the center of the representation while the urban context is assigned a visually subordinate role.

111

The Evolution of the Digital Image

Image 39

39

Christ & Gantenbein

New Fine Arts Museum Basel

Rendering
Print of the image file
in: *Bauwelt*, 101, 2010,
1/2 (8 Jan.), p. 10

1   Dietmar Steiner, "Wie die Bauwelt jetzt ist…," in *Bauwelt*, 101, 2010, 1/2 (8 Jan.), p. 9.

2   Herbert Kiefer, "Renderverbot. Wie man im Saarland die Chancengleichheit bei Wettbewerben erhöhen will," in *Bauwelt*, 101, 2010, 11 (12 Mar.), pp. 12–13, here p. 12.

3   Hubertus Adam, "Erweiterung Kunstmuseum Basel," in *Bauwelt*, 101, 2010, 1/2 (8 Jan.), pp. 10–12, here p. 10.

As the 2000s give way to the 2010s, a certain weariness of the digital architectural image becomes noticeable in the journals. Dietmar Steiner is being thoroughly critical when looking back over the "changes in the journalistic milieu of architecture since the eighties" in his article for the centenary of *Bauwelt* in issue 1/2 dated January 2010 when he says:

"And then there were the images that suddenly achieved total mastery over architectural journalists. During the last century, until the end of the 80s, architectural magazines were monochrome leaden deserts of printer's ink with many drawings and insipid images. Then in the nineties, architecture became an industrialized cultural lifestyle, and the development of celebrity star architects began, also attracting the attention of all the other forms of media. […] The Internet is awash with all sorts of architecture porn, with an enormous number of horny images and zero information."[1]

The article "Renderverbot von Saarbrücken" in issue 11 of the same year comments: two architectural competitions would dispense with the so-called "Liberoblatt," the brief description of the design idea in text and images, and the "jury would make its judgment based exclusively on drawings and models"—"renderings were not allowed."[2]

This illustration, on the other hand, could be somewhat of a counter-thesis to Steiner's remarks. This fully digital representation with minimal inserted parts of the image is not a photorealistic representation persuasively staging the future building in a supposedly material everyday situation or in an emotionally charged atmosphere. Its aim lies less in achieving the most realistic portrayal of a setting and much more in developing a specific architectural statement about the design itself from its principal characteristics. These are, on the one hand, the color and texture of the gray brick facade, which appears to resolve itself from dark to light in line with the height above ground, and, on the other hand, the special cuboid shape of the building "in the transition between St. Alban-Vorstadt and Dufourstrasse,"[3] with its striking setback corner forming a plaza that picks up the flow of the older buildings to the right and turns it toward the Rhine bridge.

These architectural elements are made to stand out by compositional means. This is firstly an almost monochromatic representation in bluish-gray tones that become lighter from bottom to top across the full image and thus reinforce the effect of the brick facade. Only the speckles of color of the staffage interrupt the uniform color scheme. The second aspect is the abstract representation of the immediate urban space, which, although certainly taken into the picture to contextualize the design, is hinted at here only as a backdrop and forms a stark contrast to the detailed reproduction of the brickwork pattern. While the monochrome color scheme creates a homogeneous impression (→ Image 31), the contrast of detail and simplification directs the observer's attention to the important elements at the center of the image (→ Image 38). In the end, this reduction shows what it represents even more to its best advantage.

Thus the image exemplifies the creation of a subtle monumental effect by simplifying the representation and reducing the compositional means employed.

The Evolution of the Digital Image

Image 40

40

Bruno Fioretti Marquez

New Visitor Center Sanssouci Palace, Schweizerhaus

Rendering
Print of the image file
in: *Bauwelt*, 102, 2011,
24 (24 June), p. 8

1 Cf. text → Image 39.

2 Franziska Weinz, "Wahr? Unwahr? Trotzdem wahr? Blauraum Architekten stiften Verwirrung," in *Bauwelt*, 102, 2011, 44 (18 Nov.), p. 2. The next quotation: ibid.; cf. Blauraum, *wirklichwahr*, exhib. cat., Berlin 2011.

3 Jens Guthoff, "Architekturgrafik mit CAD" (*ARCH*+-Baumarkt), in *ARCH*+, 1990, 102 (Jan.), p. 89. Cf. text → Image 5.

4 Cf. text → Image 19.

While the boom of the digital image produces its first responses, and the new desire for the pictorial and vivid in architectural representation activates criticism,[1] there is an attempt to give traction to the alleged "fact that making the built increasingly less easier to distinguish from the fictional has been taken too far,"[2] such as at the 2011 exhibition "wirklichwahr" at the Aedes Architecture Forum in Berlin. However, all the "somewhat somber images" on display there in black-and-white monochrome appear to be designed to be indistinguishable to the observer. The illusion perpetuated here is that photorealistic renderings are images "which the layperson cannot differentiate from a photograph."[3] This myth spreads its influence again and again with every technical step forward in quality, without provoking habituation effects among the observers or moderating the influence of the myth in general. It is clear that the human eye is capable of being bewildered on each occasion and will have to learn to make this distinction yet again.[4]

Interestingly, at the start of the 2010s, a retreat from the then-ongoing trend toward photorealistic effects is seen in the image material of the journals as well. Taking many forms, it is a diverse phenomenon to which ascribing a quantity or date is difficult, and which is better described as a general trend than a style. What can be seen is that the quantity of glaring white, light-flooded, transparent milky, and airy representations (→ Image 33) clearly declines from the start of the 2010s, and in their place comes a new, photorealistic realism that accordingly dispenses with glaring light effects, over-illumination, overexposure, and glare, as well as out-of-focus, soft-focus, or blurred objects and people.

The depiction of overcast or heavily clouded skies takes the place of flooding an image with light, and in the same way, colors become pale, natural, earthy tones, while the overall impression of the image is able to assume a discreet, subdued character extending even to a stolid, tranquil yet, at the same time, realistically refined photorealism that appears almost to be a compositional counter-thesis to the glaring white style. This reserved mood is found sporadically in the journals by the middle of the 2000s and is represented right up to the end of the study period as a facet of the design repertoire of the digital architectural image.

The image shown here is one such example but does not represent the whole of the trend. The rendered design is carefully inserted into a photograph of the site of the imagined building. In the same way as the design is adjusted in terms of its language of form, materiality, and color to the genius loci shaped by history and the passage of time, its representation is also integrated subtly into the image. This approach is apparent in the image in the way the strong sunlight in the foreground of the photograph is reproduced much less intensively in the rendered new build so that, at first glance, the design hardly attracts the eye. The integration is made still more complete by the shared beige tones, which harmonize with the rest of the fall colors. That the author has dispensed with photorealistic image effects is also shown by the frottage-like appearance of the sky, which, on closer inspection, is reminiscent of the canvas of an oil painting. As this illustration makes clear, the type of representation needs to suit the specific character of the future building (→ Image 44).

115

Image 41

41

léonwohlhage

"The Seven" Residential Complex Gärtnerplatz District Munich

Visualization:
Büro STEINLEIN
Rendering
Print of the image file
in: *Bauwelt*, 103, 2012,
36 (21 Sept.), p. 21

1   Alexander Heintze, "Zwischen Angst und Gier," in *Bauwelt*, 103, 2012, 36 (21 Sept.), pp. 18–21, here p. 20. This is one of those extremely rare cases in which the representation of the architecture is addressed at all in the journals.

2   Cf. text → Image 27.

3   According to the headline in *Bauwelt*, 107, 2016, 33 (26 Aug.), the only issue on the theme of digital architectural representation.

While digital architectural representations involving glaring white light become less popular, and discreet images with subdued light and muted colors come to the fore (→ Image 40), a golden, warm light begins to permeate the images in the journals and goes on to establish itself as a characteristic feature of digital architectural images in the 2010s. This phenomenon is already present in the second half of the 2000s. It takes its cue from the evening twilight of the blue hour representations (→ Image 34) and eventually develops into a ubiquitous mode of composition. It is not tied to a particular time of day or season, but appears in various forms—perhaps a warm summer evening, a clear fall morning, or a gloomy winter afternoon; in natural weather situations or as an illuminated or self-illuminating building, with an additional golden shimmer covering the whole image (→ Image 45), whether in light, discreet pastel tones or saturated, strong, pasty colors.

All these various forms of appearance have one sentimental basic tone that shapes the image mood with a sort of golden primer or impregnant, sometimes subtle, sometimes eye-catching. However, light effects such as over-illumination or overexposure have not disappeared. On the contrary, the golden basic tone extends even to the back-lighting, which now dissolves its surroundings in a reddish golden color instead of gleaming white. In the journals, this development shows itself as a fluid transition from glaring white daylight to the golden, warm lighting mood that—unless it is in the blue hour (→ Image 47)—is mainly reserved for late afternoon or early evening, and finally peaks in the monumental romantic light atmosphere that emerges in the journals at the end of the 2010s (→ Image 49).

This illustration from *Bauwelt* 36/2012 is an early example of a golden light mood, with an easily discernible, thoroughly photorealistic aspiration that seeks to visually anticipate its subject as photographed reality. The whole scene is bathed in warm, golden light that is shown off to its best advantage on the leaves of the trees and is further intensified by the reflections in the surface of the water in the pond. From the illustration context, an article about the situation of the Munich real estate market, it is obvious to the observer that the aim here is less the neutral, objective simulation of the future building than the communication of a particular message. The article goes on to say: "The light mood in which the up-market residential buildings are presented is always the same: evening twilight in Munich."[1] Here as well, it is not about representing reality as accurately as possible but surpassing it pictorially and giving it aesthetic added value intended to trigger a feeling of Mediterranean flair, of beauty as an oasis of calm and peace in the middle of the city, in the minds of the target group, thus awakening their desire to buy or rent the apartments.[2]

However, this image is by no means singular. As with the other examples, design visualizations are presentation images with an explicit communicative function. They operate somewhere between marketing and the provision of information, between "staging the unbuilt—selling architecture,"[3] irrespective of how artistically or strategically they are designed.

117

Image 42

42

MOA—Miebach
Oberholzer Architekten

*ZLB State Library
Tempelhofer Feld Berlin*

Rendering
Print of the image file
in: *Bauwelt*, 104, 2013,
19 (17 May), p. 17

1   *Bauwelt*, 104, 2013: 17/18 (10
    May), p. 16; 21 (31 May), pp. 14,
    15; 36 (27 Sept.), p. 8 top and
    bottom; 46 (6 Dec.), p. 12.
    Cf. text → Image 31.

2   BS, "Vor dem Rendering. So
    schön kann Architekturdarstel-
    lung sein!," in *Bauwelt*, 104, 2013,
    22 (7 June), p. 3.

3   Cf. text → Image 39.

With the fluid transition from a glaring white to a golden, warm light and the trend of refined photorealistic realism, the digital architectural image achieves a large bandwidth of compositional and stylistic diversity in the first half of the 2010s. It must also be stressed here that it is not about fully detailed, definitive styles but significant image phenomena that can be seen in the journals and the Schinkel competition and are assigned tentatively to various categories here. The year 2013 sees the appearance of a conspicuously high number of monochrome representations as well, for example.[1] Meanwhile, the criticism of digital architectural images continues. During the same year, a *Bauwelt* review of an exhibition of architectural drawings from the twentieth century with the title "Duktus" in the Architectural Museum of the University of Applied Sciences, Berlin, provides an overview of the current image practice:

> "Most architectural representations these days are as peculiarly standardized and soulless as architectural text. What are constantly described in text as 'fluid' and 'light-flooded' spaces that 'invite the visitor to tarry' appear in the representations as eternally similar computer renderings, with more or less dramatic light moods and redundant photographs of happy John and Jane Does in the foreground."[2]

On the one hand, it becomes clear that the surfeit of rendering continues to grow.[3] On the other hand, a tendency to standardize is shown at its best in the actual practice of digital architectural representation, which is an indication that something of a representational canon of the conventional digital architectural image has now developed.

In comparison, this illustration stands out among the usual methods of representation. While it is certainly an image flooded with light, it is done in such a way that the light is made the main theme of the image. It shows the central perspective of an interior view that is made to look highly dynamic by the seemingly elliptical openings in the ceiling. The glaring white sunlight shines with such intensity through these openings, which are also in the glass facade, that large parts of the architecture are overexposed. This permits the use of a simplified representation of the geometry and allows the curved concrete bands of the ceiling opening to appear to hover in the light. The synthesizing effect is reinforced by the reduced range of colors. At the same time, the golden shimmer of the indirectly illuminated architectural components divides the image into yellowish right and bluish left halves, while the almost black, shadowed corner areas emphasize the diagonal nature of the image composition.

The rear-view depiction of a person placed centrally in the foreground, holding a shielding hand before his eyes in order not to be blinded by the backlight, adds a narrative moment (→ Image 35) to the image and helps to monumentalize the scene. The observers are inserted into a perspective in which they see a lost-looking person with a briefcase who becomes an accidental witness to an overpowering spectacle of nature taking place directly in front of him in the library building. At the same time, the architecture is elevated to a natural space and experiences an aesthetic enhancement above and beyond its actual purpose. Light used in this way as a compositional means becomes a narrative moment and is thus integrated in a meaningful manner into the image, instead of simply playing an external role in creating the desired atmosphere.

119

Image 43

43

Jonas Dahlberg

*Memorial Site
on Utøya Island,
Panorama of the Island*

Rendering
Print of the image file
in: *Bauwelt*, 105, 2014,
13 (4 April), p. 10

1   Cf. text → Image 42.

2   *Bauwelt*, 97, 2006, 9 (24 Feb.),
    p. 28 top right; *Bauwelt*, 98, 2007,
    7 (9 Feb.), p. 15.

3   *Bauwelt*, 103, 2012, 42 (2 Nov.),
    p. 10 top and middle; *Bauwelt*,
    104, 2013, 21 (31 May), p. 14.

4   Cf. text → Image 41.

As it says in the review from 2013,[1] an increasing dramatization of the light mood is noticeable in the images in the journals during the course of the 2010s. In addition to the season, the weather is an effective compositional means to orchestrate the image effect. Dramatically colored cloudy skies make an early appearance (→ Image 19) but remain the exception (→ Image 31). The first heavy rain in a rendering falls in 2006; the first gray clouds gather a year later.[2] The first truly effective atmospheric representation is the image of the Hamburg Elbphilharmonie (→ Image 36). Renderings that are not blue hour or evening mood are usually fine weather situations, with or without white clouds in a bright-blue sky, or there is no weather at all.

The discovery of the natural atmosphere of the weather as a means of shaping the aesthetic "atmosphere" of the image can be said to begin only from the first half of the 2010s. The first umbrella is put up in 2012, the first flame-red sky appears in 2013, but these are infrequent exceptions.[3] Taking the evening sky of the blue hour and the overcast sky of refined photorealism (→ Image 30 and 40) as the starting point, there are now images in which the golden evening mood is often given a dramatic, threatening accent by heavy, dark clouds gathering ahead of rain or a storm, and the depicted weather conditions vary much more strongly in general. Dark weather is not infrequently a compositional opportunity for more light. Wet surfaces, for example, allow the depiction of additional light reflections and mirroring. Glaring light through a hole in the clouds appears to be more intense. Above all, however, naturally dark lighting situations allow a building to be staged as illuminated or self-illuminated at any time of day and not just during the evening hours (→ Image 45). As with the golden, warm light,[4] this tendency also leads to the type of monumental atmospheric light effect that appears in the journals toward the end of the 2010s (→ Image 49).

The image makes clear in an exemplary manner that the dramatic light mood is also being used to articulate an intended statement pictorially. The illustration shows the design by the Swedish artist Jonas Dahlberg for the memorial to the victims murdered on July 22, 2011, in a terrorism incident on the Norwegian island of Utøya near Oslo. The design envisages a channel cut through the rock of the island with the names of the sixty-nine dead engraved on its walls. This event is so dreadful that it is barely conceivable. By the same token, the design cannot be depicted like an ordinary building or structure. Instead, this is an attempt to let the authentic place speak for itself through an overwhelming photograph of nature, which looks as if it has been painted and shows the planned intervention as causing as little disturbance as possible: at the center of the image is the monumental drama of the somber, overcast natural scene, which is intended to transfer from the photograph to the design, which itself appears to disappear into the image.

The image is a further example of the great influence the photograph of the project surroundings can have on the image effect, achieved with a photomontage (→ Image 21, 29, 34, and 37).

121

Image 44

44

Staab Architekten

Bauhaus Archive Extension Berlin, Interior Perspective

Visualization:
Sönke Reteike
(Staab Architekten)
Rendering
Print of the image file
in: *Bauwelt*, 106, 2015,
43 (13 Nov.), p. 12

1   *ARCH+* 171/2004 (June) is the
    first issue to be in color. Only one
    previous exception: *ARCH+* 2001,
    154/155 (Jan.).

2   *Bauwelt*, 102, 2011, 6 (4 Feb.),
    p. 10 middle.

3   Cf. text → Image 40.

As this image exemplifies, black-and-white representations renew their presence in the 2010s in journals from which they had more or less previously disappeared. Black-and-white illustrations are a special form of monochrome (→ Image 31) and constitute a significant topos. They represent both a widespread standard of printing technology and a historical epoch of photography and film, as well as being associated in a special way with historicity. Collective presentations of the past frequently consist of black-and-white photographs such as memories of personal family histories. In addition, black and white represents an abstraction of perception that does not correspond with human vision. It creates a distancing effect between the observer and the subject of the photograph, in somewhat the same way—albeit in reverse—that the later coloration of old films or photographs attempts to reach for a closer connection to earlier events. Black-and-white illustrations have a specific aesthetic quality that also carries with it great semantic significance.

Publishing black-and-white reproductions of—often originally colored—digital images remains current practice in the journals until the 2000s (→ Image 6, 10, and 15). *ARCH+* appears on the shelves in black and white until 2004.[1] In *Bauwelt* as well, it is the middle of the 2000s before color images take the place of black and white, which then suddenly disappears from the competition section. The first black-and-white image to reappear there does so in 2011.[2] Black and white is evidently taboo in the boom years of the digital image.

The few black-and-white design visualizations that appear sporadically from then on deliberately dispense with color in order to use black and white as a compositional medium of style. This is also the case with this fully digital representation, in which there are very few inserted staffage elements and even the surroundings are rendered. As can be seen in particular in the area of the concrete floor, dispensing with polychromy is very conducive to producing a photorealistic, almost tangible material effect. In general, use of a single color in large amounts promotes a homogeneous impression of the image. A good thirty years separate the existing building and the extension, but the ensemble appears so uniformly consistent that they could have been cast from the same mold. The new connects to the old in its pictorial anticipation of its future state to form a harmonized whole. This impression is strengthened by the associated proximity of the black-and-white mode to the historical specifics of the building's role as a memorial site for the "architecture of the modern age," which in the imagination is essentially characterized by the reception of black-and-white photographs. The visualization takes up this reference—not least with a humorous wink by adding that architect whose legacy is documented here for posterity to the staffage at the far left.

This image also exemplifies the compositional claim to create a mode of visualization that corresponds to the specific character of the building's purpose and expresses it in a clear and vivid way.[3]

123

The Evolution of the Digital Image

Image 45

45

Atelier 30 Architekten

Gallery Building Steidl Göttingen

Visualization:
Martinez-Noel, 3D WAY
Architectural Graphics
Rendering
Print of the image file
in: *Bauwelt*, 107, 2016,
21 (27 May), p. 16

1   Cf. text → Image 33 and 41.

2   Friederike Meyer in conversation with Christoph Reichen and Malte Kloes from bildbau, in *Bauwelt*, 107, 2016, 33 (26 Aug.), pp. 26–29, here p. 28.

3   Sebastian Redecke, "Steidls Galerie für Göttingen," in *Bauwelt*, 107, 2016, 21 (27 May), pp. 14–17, here p. 16.

As already mentioned,[1] the special issue "Ungebautes inszenieren—Architektur verkaufen" appears in Bauwelt 33 in August 2016. It is the only one of the journal's special issues to cover the digital image as a medium for architectural representation between 1980 and 2020. The topic is otherwise hardly discussed in the journals or explicitly treated as a subject for debate in any other way. Like the topic of architectural representation in general, the digital image remains strangely unreflected throughout the entire period—in stark contrast to its omnipresence in architectural practice. This makes the interviews with professional external visualization agencies all the more revealing. They offer extremely rare insights into the practice of digital image creation. Malte Kloes and Christoph Reichen answer the central question about what goes into making the image mood:

"[CR] The light mood has the greatest influence on the image mood. Light and shadow define the basic atmosphere of the image and are the main tools for staging the materiality of the architecture. [...] [MK] Our images are mostly collages of renderings and photographs. Bringing together the different media into one image in such a way as to produce coherence is an art. Brightness, contrast, and color determine the overall composition. Desaturation allows everything to come together better automatically."[2]

The two visualizers are thus addressing important aspects that are also to be found in this illustration. Much of what became clear in the previous examples can be understood here. In addition to the principle of the photomontage (→ Image 21), it is above all the trend to create monochrome representations by reducing the color spectrum of the photograph of the project's surroundings, like the warm brown tones of the rendered design, that create a visual alignment of photograph and rendering (→ Image 31). In this case, it is monochromization rather than desaturation that allows "everything to come together better automatically." This homogenization effect is considerably strengthened by the golden light mood, probably created with a semitransparent color filter, that covers the whole image like a veil and culminates in the shimmering warm light shining out of the entrance area of the building (→ Image 34 and 41). At the same time, the image seems careful not to let the golden glow get out of hand, and recaptures it to some extent with the muted earthy tones and the overcast sky. From that point of view, a certain discreet tendency is also to be seen here (→ Image 40), even though the scene is additionally dramatized by the depicted weather, with its heavy clouds and subdued sunlight (→ Image 43). People have also been added into the image of Düstere Straße (Somber Street), where the design is to be realized.

The image seems to be adapted to the materiality and color of the tamped concrete facade, into which "small lighting elements in the form of acrylic tubes are recessed in some places," allowing "messages in word or abstract image form to be projected outward."[3] The facade is therefore the main building element. Overall, the design appears in its pictorial staging as an attractive, magical place, a kind of "ark" in the Göttingen town center that strikes the observer as both hermetic and inviting. The beams of light from the sky falling in the direction of the seemingly hollowed-out, illuminated entrance, the birds flying above the building, and its ship-like appearance graphically narrate and further extend this association (→ Image 35).

125

Image 46

46

Max Rudolph,
Nikita Suerhoff

Schinkel Competition 2016

Rendering
Print of the digital copy
Architectural Museum
TU Berlin, Inv. No. SW-A
2016, 01- 02

1   Cf. text → Image 40.

2   BS, "Vor dem Rendering. So schön kann Architekturdarstellung sein!," in *Bauwelt*, 104, 2013, 22 (7 June), p. 3.

3   Herbert Kiefer, "Renderverbot. Wie man im Saarland die Chancengleichheit bei Wettbewerben erhöhen will," in *Bauwelt*, 101, 2010, 11 (12 Mar.), pp. 12–13.

4   Friederike Meyer in conversation with Christoph Reichen and Malte Kloes from bildbau, in *Bauwelt*, 107, 2016, 33 (26 Aug.), pp. 26–29, here p. 26. This is with reference to explicit renderings.

5   Marcel Bächtiger, "Lockere Präzision," 7.5.2015 <https://www.hochparterre.ch/nachrichten/wettbewerbe/lockere-praezision//> (last accessed 30.1.2024).

6   Stan Allen, "Endgeschwindigkeiten: Der Computer im Entwurfs-Studio," in *ARCH+*, 1995, 128 (Sept.), pp. 58–62.

7   Reader's comment on Bächtiger, "Lockere Präzision."

8   Friederike Meyer in conversation with Justus Ettemeyer of EVE images, in *Bauwelt*, 107, 2016, 33 (26 Aug.), pp. 22–25, here p. 23.

9   Cf. text → Image 33.

The criticism of the digital architectural image[1] and the "eternally similar computer renderings"[2] appears at the beginning of the 2010s in the journals and continues in the second half of the same decade. The "Renderverbot von Saarbrücken"[3] article is by no means a one-off instance of renderings being banned, with *Bauwelt* 33/2016 stating on the topic of rendering that it is "now often heard that images are limited or even forbidden in competitions."[4] This raises the question "to what extent such a formal rejection is in fact sensible or merely the upshot of a forthright, fashionable aversion to renderings"[5] in other media contexts as well. A frequently heard answer is the argument put forward in 1995 by Stan Allen involving the "distance between the thing and its representation,"[6] according to which the "hastily forced image, that […] suggests the finished building, […] greatly endangers the openness of architects to allow their own work to mature to fruition."[7] The visualizer Justus Ettemeyer of EVE images, in the previously mentioned *Bauwelt* issue, states that liability for information provided in a prospectus will become increasingly important with digital architectural images, "because the images are becoming increasingly realistic."[8]

The focus of the criticism is therefore the accusation that the photorealistic architectural image, being a mixture of a supposedly factual, true-to-reality representation and an intended, persuasive emotional effect, could interrupt the iterative process of design at too early a stage and hinder the full development of the architectural potential by anticipating the design too early as the seemingly photographed completed state of the project.

This presentation image from the Schinkel competition in 2016 demonstrates that "images are becoming increasingly realistic," even in this architectural image produced by undergraduate students.[9] The gentian-blue water in the sharp-edged swimming pool, already surrealistically depicted, contrasts with the fading landscape dissolving in the mist. However, the boundary between montage and rendering is difficult to detect because all the areas retain their liveliness through light and materiality. Image and rendering merge into an atmospheric ensemble of extraordinary freshness that is intended to emphasize the experiential character of the building project. In the end, it is the confinement of the mist effect to the top half of the image that gives it away as a montage.

Thus the image is an indication that, during the 2010s, images become "increasingly realistic," but at the same time, unrealistic scenes can be depicted as photorealistic using digital visualization tools to such an extent that they undermine their own realistic effect: the type of representation looks deceptively real, but the depicted scene is perceived as unreal or even surreal. Here it is a conflicting coincidence of a summerlike warm bathing scene and the damp cold of foggy weather, while at the same time the lighting, which appears to come from several sources and, undoubtedly, appropriately stages the design, does not quite correspond with any real, natural situation.

The Evolution of the Digital Image

Image 47

47

C.F. Møller Architects /
Beauty & the Bit
(Visualization)

*Via University College
Campus Horsens*

Rendering
Print of the image file
in: *Bauwelt*, 108, 2017,
22 (3 Nov.), p. 15

1   Cf. text → Image 40.

2   Cf. e.g. *Bauwelt*, 99, 2008,
     43 (14 Nov.), p. 26; *Bauwelt*, 107,
     2016, 31 (12 Aug.), p. 16; *Bauwelt*,
     110, 2019, 16 (9 Aug.), p. 23.

Another reason why digital architectural images appear "increasingly realistic" may have something to do with a development in the field of photography rather than that of rendering. In the 2010s, while the trend toward ever more perfect realistic representation continues in computer graphics with concepts such as "CGI" (Computer-Generated Imagery), the reverse is observed in digital photography with concepts such as "HDRI" (High Dynamic Range Image), with the photographic image distancing itself stylistically from its traditional appearance and moving in the direction of an image aesthetic that is in some ways artificial-looking. The two types of imagery, digitally generated images and digital photographic representations, are coming closer to one another. The boundaries between the pair begin to blur.

With the introduction of image processing software such as Photoshop, it is possible to use the same digital tools in both spheres, with the result that it is valid in practical terms to speak of a convergence of computer graphics and photography. The difficulty in telling the difference between photograph and rendering cannot merely be attributed to the increasing realism of the digital image. This is also due to the fact that photography as the reference medium for the digital photorealism is rapidly approaching the aesthetic of the digital image.[1]

This convergence is intensified in the journals by the leveling effect of the printed image. *Bauwelt* contains quite a number of illustrations that look like renderings but are in fact photographs according to the information given. They are therefore not clearly identifiable as one or the other[2]—signs of changes in the observer's habitual ways of perception.

Even with this image, it is not easy to tell the difference between rendering and photograph, at least for the untrained eye. The difference between computer-generated elements and inserted photographic staffage does not show unless the object is examined using a magnifying glass or by zooming in. Several factors are at work here to create this impression. The first is the special blue hour moment (→ Image 30), which generates further effects to the benefit of the impression created by the image. In lighting terms, the blue hour is a reduction of the color spectrum like that which occurs in nature; to a certain extent it is a natural tendency toward monochrome (→ Image 31), accompanied by a darkening of the image. Colors also diminish with the disappearing daylight. Objects, such as the yellowish red brick facade of the building, no longer appear in their own color but in darker shades of blue that connect well with the intensive blue of the sky. In a similar way to the golden light mood (→ Image 34 and 41), the whole image is bathed in a uniform hue. This reduces the number of details, which are otherwise extremely precisely reproduced and yet do not spoil the homogeneous overall impression (→ Image 31). The artificial lighting in turn harmonizes with the color palette of the blue hour, in the same way as the pink and turquoise in the illuminated stories of the taller building.

This image makes clear how the realistic impression can be enhanced if the aim of achieving a naturalistic portrayal is set to one side and the visualization is simplified in a plausible manner by exploiting a natural light situation. The blue hour here reveals its persuasive effect, with a hint of Mediterranean dolce vita on the Danish Baltic Sea coast.

129

Image 48

48

Monadnock

Atlas House Eindhoven (8th Wienerberger Brick Award), Exterior Elevation

Rendering
Print of the image file
in: *Bauwelt*, 109, 2018,
15 (27 July), p. 59

1   Cf. text → Image 35, 39, 42, and 46.

2   *Bauwelt*, 101, 2010, 29 (30 July), p. 11; *Bauwelt*, 102, 2011, 20 (20 May), pp. 14, 16; *Bauwelt*, 104, 2013, 47 (13 Dec.), p. 11.

3   See Fig. 2 in the contribution from Florian Henrich, p. 33.

4   Olivier Meystre, "Hand in Hand: analog und digital," in *Bauwelt*, 108, 2017, 24 (1 Dec.), pp. 60–63, here p. 63.

5   Cf. text → Image 25, 29, 38, and 46.

With the reversal of the rendering boom into a weariness with the "enormous number of fabulous images" and "eternally similar computer renderings,"[1] increasing signs of a conscious rejection of the conventional photorealistic rendering and more of a willingness to search for alternative approaches to digital architectural representation are found in the journals from the mid-2010s. These sorts of approaches to computer graphics were already being referred to around the year 2000 as "Non-Photorealistic Rendering" (NPR). Following the reintroduction of the first drawings from the start of the 2010s,[2] however, non-photorealistic visualizations do not become a significant phenomenon in *Bauwelt* and *ARCH+* until the second half of the same decade. Interestingly, this occurs in parallel with the increasing popularity of the golden light mood (→ Image 34 and 41), even though quantitatively at a much lower level.[3]

This rejection is described using terms such as "post-digital drawing" and is manifested both by a return to the form of the collage (→ Image 50) and by dispensing with typical features of photorealistic image composition, for example illumination models that imitate realistic light situations or complex texturing of surfaces that uses mapping to simulate the appearance of materials. Instead of photographic simulations, image composition is now oriented toward graphical processes and is evident through its flat colors. Light and shadow are shown using lighter and darker tones, while textures and objects are highly simplified in their depiction. This form of digital design representation is rather more trendy, bold, and simple than schematic and abstract.

The spectrum of graphical approaches is broad: everything from borrowing ideas from painting and drawing to watercolor and hybrid representations "that may well have first been drawn by hand on paper but are subsequently scanned, duplicated and rearranged on the computer screen."[4] This approach would also include distancing or minimizing the photorealistic impression by effects such as frottage (→ Image 40). In one respect they are all the same: they are not intended to anticipate the finally built object as persuasively as a photograph, but rather to offer up a closed, illusionistic pictorial effect and stage the design as something provisional, possible, and designable, exposing its character in the form of an image construction.[5]

This illustration may be representative of the abundance of such alternative approaches to image design. As is easy to recognize, it completely distances itself in appearance from the usual digital design representations. Despite the reduced, two-dimensional style of the image, it looks as animated as the brick facade at its center. In addition, the design appears more two- than three-dimensional, with the three-dimensionality being suggested in the front elevation only by the shadow throw. The completely monochrome, surreal background intensifies this effect. The texturing of the facade looks as graphic as the trees, hedges, and bushes, whose photographic origins are now largely disguised after digital post-processing, and combines everything into a coherent image effect that complements the calm composition of the design. References to naive paintings and fauvism come to mind, as do woodcuts and poster art.

131

The Evolution of the Digital Image

Image 49

49

Henning Larsen Architects, Topotek 1

Redesign of Esbjerg Bypark

Rendering
Print of the image file
in: *Bauwelt*, 110, 2019,
17 (23 Aug.), p. 16

1   For an early example of a rendering based on painting, see *Bauwelt*, 97, 2006, 43 (10 Nov.), pp. 20/21.

2   Marie Bruun Yde, "Ein Bild von einem Park," in *Bauwelt*, 110, 2019, 17 (23 Aug.), pp. 16–18, here p. 18.

3   Chris Dähne, "Die 'analogen Bilder' digitaler Architektur," in *Wolkenkuckucksheim*, 25, 2021, 40, pp. 113–24.

Whereas a clear turn away from the conventional photorealism of digital architectural representation can be seen from the second half of the 2010s (→ Image 48), more recent times have seen how the golden light mood (→ Image 34 and 41) intensifies into the dramatic, monumental pathos of an overpoweringly romantic light atmosphere. This does not refer to some directed course of development of the digital architectural image, but more to a further compositional trend that begins to emerge in the journals toward the end of the 2010s and appears to originate in Scandinavia. Because such images are a relatively rare occurrence, their effect is all the more imposing.[1]

The image opposite makes this clear in a descriptive manner in the case of the design for a city park in a Danish port produced by a Danish architectural practice jointly with a German firm of landscape architects. The image is so unusual and opulent that the style of the design itself becomes a matter of comment, something that is extremely unusual in the journals:

"The Bypark competition gives the opportunity to focus a little more closely on graphical representation as evidenced by these extraordinary painting-like perspectives by Topotek 1 and Henning Larsens. The images successfully emphasize the atmosphere of the various areas within their design and in this way differentiate between the individual amenity spaces. The almost over-the-top painting style reminiscent of Caspar David Friedrich could be intended to be an art historical reference. Whatever the case may be, it refreshingly sets itself apart from the customary glossy urban life illustrations generally found in competition entries and, in a certain way, fits particularly well with the concept of the park. It remains open to question whether the powerful image is in the right place—Esbjerg is neither large nor romantic. Esbjerg is raw."[2]

As is clearly noticeable here, the compositional staging does not rely on the blue hour mode (→ Image 30 and 47), but rather on a dramatic light scene (→ Image 43) of the kind frequently observed after a storm, when the sun breaks through the clouds, or at sea during some quickly changing weather conditions. Standing in front of the rusty railings in the image foreground, which are obviously part of the existing surroundings, the observers transform here as well into viewers, who participate almost inadvertently in the overwhelming spectacle of nature happening before them in the park (→ Image 42). The image section is defined such that the observer's view is nearly blinded by the glaring backlight, which communicates its intensity indexically through the contrast of light and shadow on the old water tower.

The greatest source of astonishment may be that the computer-generated image has none of the typical features of a photorealistic rendering. Completely without luster, reflections, and transparency, it succeeds in appearing almost like a romantic oil painting. Subject and motif: landscape, clouds, light contribute to this impression, as do the high resolution and the absence of any copy-and-paste redundancies, even in the vegetation. In this respect, it suggests that the "art historical reference" is quite intentional, as has already been established for contemporary architectural image practice.[3] Irrespective of the question of the genius loci, the park design appears in this staging as precisely what it is: an artificially created and artistically designed natural space.

133

Image 50

50

Johannes Hertell

Schinkel Competition 2019

Digital collage
Print of the digital copy
Architectural Museum
TU Berlin, no Inv. No.

1   Cf. e.g. *Bauwelt*, 103, 2012, 36 (21 Sept.), pp. 58, 59; *Bauwelt*, 105, 2014, 23 (13 June), p. 11 top.

In addition to the deliberate dispensing with the typical features of photorealistic architectural representation (→ Image 48), the turning away from conventional rendering is mainly expressed through an increased recourse to the principle of the collage (→ Image 16, 22, and 25). Just like the digital "art historical reference" (→ Image 49), the search for alternative approaches to image composition is heavily influenced by ideas and methods from the analog age. However, even in digital oil painting images that dispense with the typical photorealistic features, the closed form of the illusionistic image is retained. Into the place of the imitation of photography steps the imitation of painting.

By comparison, the renewed emergence of the collage from the second half of the 2010s marks the revival of a digital image form from the turn of the millennium (→ Image 25), which, despite now being imitated only as a style,[1] is revisited as a matter of course in order to playfully visualize a first idea, a first architectural concept, or a social vision, instead of simulating a real situation as realistically as possible. An open, non-persuasive form of image, in which the objects are set in the scene as something yet to be designed, is undergoing a revival through the collage. The two features—the turning away from conventional photorealism and the emphasizing of the open, collage-like character—frequently occur together in practice, but are also found on their own. Real photographic elements are often placed in digital collages as well in the second half of the 2010s (→ Image 48).

Last but not least, the emergence of alternative digital approaches to image composition is also dependent on the type and purpose of the project, who commissions the work, the chosen architectural practice, and, crucially in every case, its attitude to design. It is noticeable that the alternative approaches to image composition, such as those increasingly found in journals from the middle of the 2010s, as a rule have an "alternative" project background and are adopted by smaller, less well-financed but socially and ecologically minded offices.

Alternative approaches are also found in image material for the Schinkel competition, such as this image, toward the end of the observation period of the study. Here there are a number of levels—the line drawing together with the pastel pencil–generated color plane or the inserted photograph of the couple dancing—creating a poetic whole with their open composition. The individual levels come fully into play and offer the dancing performance a key role in the image as well as a stage. An unambiguous boundary to the image is deliberately avoided. The unfinished look of the side areas draws attention to the image design. This is the basis for the image composition. However, the architecture also remains on an abstract design level that appears here as a vague spatial vision, as an idea still to be defined and left open to interpretation.

The Evolution of the Digital Image

Image 51

51

HPP Architekten

*New Facade on a Tower
on Riebeckplatz in Halle
an der Saale, Cross-Section
Perspective*

Visualization:
bloomimages
Rendering
Print of the image file
in: *Bauwelt*, 111, 2020,
10 (15 May), p. 21

1   Cf. text → Image 35.

This image brings to a close the forty-year period of observation of the practice of digital architectural representation between 1980 and 2020. It dates from the year 2020, only half of which could be examined for project logistics reasons. However, even these first six months include a multitude of high-quality, complex, rich, and sometimes magnificent renderings. These types of image occur increasingly frequently and appear to establish themselves as the new standard for digital architectural representation. While the number of digital images achieves its absolute maximum of a good 140 visualizations in *Bauwelt* by 2018,[1] starting from the digital image boom in the second half of the 2000s, a significant improvement in rendering quality becomes evident in the course of the 2010s. Due to the technical development of digital tools, this is above all in the visualization of light and lighting as an integrative means for producing the image syntheses.

This tendency continues until the end of the 2010s. Quality standards rise still further. However, this is not accompanied by any new, significant image design trends. The pages of the journals during the first half of 2020 carry examples of emotive, dramatic, and romantic light atmospheres as well as the continuing boom of the golden light mood and the blue hour. There are also examples of clouds, mist, and storms as the means of creating atmospheric drama, monochrome representations, photorealistically designed surreal scenes, a large number of illusionistic images, and, in one case, an alternative approach in the form of a trendy collage.

Against the background of the status quo of digital design visualization at the start of the 2020s, with its continuing predominant paradigm of photorealistic illusionism, this image is rather atypical. It denotes a rare case in which the compositional means of a digital architectural image are not used to make the design appear as realistic as possible, but instead to make the real world better understandable visually through the use of unrealistic interventions. Unlike the surreal depiction of real subjects (→ Image 46), the focus here is less on achieving an aesthetic effect than on creating a didactic moment. The image connects the epistemic potential of a section of a building to the aesthetic mood of a photorealistic rendering that is inserted into a real photograph. The viewers are thus placed in an impossible perspective, in a position where they could never stand. This virtual setting, showing the world like this, realistically but cut open, is combined with unrealistic physical material properties. For example, the inner glass facade should be reflective when viewed from such an oblique angle, but it is shown as transparent, revealing the person wearing the tie. This is conspicuous because reflections elsewhere in the image are depicted very accurately. The aim here is to avoid a tunnel-like view of the intermediate green zone of the facade, which is designed as a winter garden, and instead to enable an overall view that unites three main aspects—the facade construction, the excellent facilities to sit or linger within the building, and its integration into the urban context via the panoramic view over the city—in a single overall perspective.

The image therefore fulfills not only a communicative but also an informative function that goes beyond its suggestive character. This is also a way to successfully combine vividness and abstraction. Of course, the atmospheric golden light mood was chosen here as well.

137

Hubert Locher

Images for Consumption: Message and Rhetoric of the Digital Architectural Image

1   Alexander Geringer, "Editorial," in *H.O.M.E.*, 2020, 1 (Jan.), [p. 9].

2   Interview with Lars Krückeberg, Wolfram Putz, and Thomas Willemeit from GRAFT Architekten, in *H.O.M.E.*, 2020, 1 (Jan.), pp. 72–82, here p. 82.

3   Website GRAFT Gesellschaft von Architekten <https://graftlab.com/about> (last accessed 19.1.2024).

4   In fact, this virtual construct already existed. There is a comprehensive list of projects in chronological order on the architects' website. A search based on the characteristics of the H.O.M.E. Haus finds it as Villa J, which is listed with a date of 2015 and the status "design." See <https://graftlab.com/projects/villa-j> (last accessed 29.1.2024).

Fig. 1: Title page of the article "Das HOME 2020," *H.O.M.E.*, 2020, 1 (Jan.), p. 67

To celebrate its twentieth anniversary, the January 2020 issue of the magazine *H.O.M.E.*—which, as "the design magazine for well-being," is aimed at a broad public interested in architecture and design—proudly presents "Das Haus 2020!" (Fig. 1). The editorial says: "In this issue, we are delighted to present the first master case for living culture: H.O.M.E. Haus 2020 by GRAFT Architekten." They would have "designed a state-of-the-art villa for H.O.M.E. All the processes for building and completing the H.O.M.E. Haus 2020 are shown in this issue."[1]

Paging further through the issue reveals all kinds of views of an extremely generously designed detached house surrounded by various forms of greenery. Situated on sloping ground at the foot of a vineyard, the building has a green roof and is evidently constructed in an ecologically considerate manner. The reader is informed about the earthworks, the ground floor slab with perimeter insulation, and the walls, which are of earthen construction. The architectural team is introduced and shown in a project meeting in the Berlin office. It is held that one would have learned about teamwork by singing in a choir during his studies at Braunschweig, that one is not subject to the "rule of the right angle" in one's own design office, which is obviously the case here with the "Haus 2020." Finally, the magazine takes a look at all the interior fittings and furnishings of the house—which, of course, as described in the editorial as well, are also "curated" by the H.O.M.E. editorial team. On closer inspection, however, the observer feels somewhat confused; the image is too beautiful, too complete. After one reads the full interview with the architects, it transpires that the "house in southern England [...] was in the end not built"[2] and the presentation is a complete fiction—or, better, a piece of virtual architecture.

However, the components of the interior fittings and the architectural team are real. GRAFT Architekten is an extremely successful architectural office set up in 1998 in Los Angeles by Lars Krückeberg, Wolfram Putz, and Thomas Willemeit. It now has branches in Los Angeles, Berlin, and Shanghai. On its attractive website, the firm styles itself as a "studio for architecture, urban planning, design, music, and the pursuit of happiness." In 2014, the practice broadens its activities by adding Graft Brandlab to provide consultancy services in the field of design for communication and brand strategy. One slogan connects the two parts of the company: "Building Spatial Identities."[3] The products are, on the one hand, houses made of stone, steel, and glass; on the other, virtual spaces—communication spaces, aesthetic living environments, brands.

H.O.M.E. Haus 2020 shows how both intertwine.[4] Everything this architectural office accomplishes here is done to a high standard, even when not considered to be its main task: to create architecture that is as convincing "as an image." Architecture is practiced as an aesthetic game. The power to create convincing reality wins this game by seamlessly connecting fiction to real people and objects. There was apparently a "client in southern England" who, it is said, lives "in an old, former bishop's palace dating from the Fin de Siècle" and wanted a new home for reasons of energy efficiency. So there is also a plot of land of the right quality and facing in a specific direction, new technology, which is also subsequently discussed in the magazine, and furnishings and fittings. However, above all else, there is the public, the target group, the potential consumers for all these products and services.

139

Images for Consumption

5   On this differentiation cf. Horst Bredekamp, "Leibniz' Reflexion von Vitruvs Ichnographia und Scaenographia," in *Vitruvianism: Origins and Transformations*, ed. Paolo Sanvito, Berlin and Boston 2015, pp. 13–18.

6   A good example is the competition design by Filippo Juvara for the Concorso Clementino der Accademia di San Luca in Rome, which contains a captivating bird's-eye perspective of the planned building. See *Von Bernini bis Piranesi. Römische Architekturzeichnungen des Barock*, ed. Elisabeth Kieven, exhib. cat. Graphical collection of the Stuttgart state gallery, Stuttgart 1993, cat. no. 70, pp. 200–201; quill and brown ink, gray wash on brownish paper, 471×1084 mm, Staatliche Museen zu Berlin, Kunstbibliothek hand drawing 1151.

7   Cf. Rolf Sachsse, *Bild und Bau. Zur Nutzung technischer Medien beim Entwerfen von Architektur*, Berlin and Boston 2000; Hubert Locher and Rolf Sachsse (ed.), *Architektur Fotografie. Darstellung—Verwendung—Gestaltung*, Berlin and Munich 2016.

Rhetorical images

Without doubt, this particular example is a special situation. *H.O.M.E.* is a magazine and not a professional journal for creators of architecture. Here architecture is made the surroundings for the presentation of consumer goods, for advertising. The atmosphere is more important than the design; it is all about the impression of an environment, the perception of life that is communicated with a space, in this case with a fictional building. This suggests that these images are created as part of a traditional task in the field of architectural representation. They are perspective views of a type that has always been submitted for competitions, where it would be supplemented by actual drawings, to give an anticipatory impression of the effect of a building before it has been built.

Therefore, the explicit differentiation from the rendering, the illusionistic representation based on design data and photography—in this specific case, the computer visualization of an intended built object in the real world for the purposes of presenting the object—is also not the topmost interest for GRAFT Architekten. Not that there are any secrets being kept here. The difference is unimportant, because it is designs and not-yet-built houses that are presented, in other words objects, all of which architects have designed, and not structures constructed by bricklayers and engineers. No lies, no deception here. People rely on the rhetoric of illusionistic representation as evidence of appearance: what can be presented as realistic or illusionistic is believable. What can be shown as if it were built, what appears as if it already exists, can also be built.

Architecture has always been reliant on the image as a means of communication. Before anything can be built, it must be planned—in other words, an image of what is to be built must be designed. These images of planned buildings can only be abstractions, the degree of abstraction being very variable. Many sources affirm that several image modes have always existed alongside one another and were used for this purpose. Vitruvius, whose architectural treatise has been interpreted and adapted since the fifteenth century, differentiates between plan (ichnographia), elevation (orthographia), and perspective view (scaenographia). While the first two are orthogonal representations, the third is the natural, three-dimensional view. Accordingly, interpretations of Vitruvius see his ichnographia as the quasi-godlike view of something and his scaenographia as the human view of an object, and they are assigned two completely different means of perception.[5] In the eighteenth century, the ostensibly human view—or, better, the illusionistic, three-dimensional, vivified representation—experiences a special rise in often virtuoso presentation drawings.[6] In the twentieth century, attempts are made to include that technology which, as an imaging process, requires a given material reality and is therefore also used as evidence: the photograph.[7] However, the photograph is an image created after the event and stands in sharp contrast to the design as the imagined image. For example, photographically represented elements of a given reality are placed in the form of a collage in the visualization in a graphically abstract manner in order to integrate elements of reality pictorially, as it were, and to highlight the relationship and differences

140

Hubert Locher

8   *Mies van der Rohe—Montage, Collage*, ed. Andreas Beitin, Wolf Eiermann, and Brigitte Franzen, exhib. cat. Ludwig Forum Aachen 2016 and Museum Georg Schäfer, Cologne 2017.

9   See the contribution from Dominik Lengyel and Catherine Toulouse, pp. 10–19.

at the same time; the collages of Mies van der Rohe should be mentioned here.[8] This aesthetic view subsequently also shows in architectural photography, which strives to represent this approach with strict objectivity. Since the end of the twentieth century, the use of digital image technologies can be added to the above insofar as they accommodate the latent need for illusionistic visualization with technical means on a new level: they allow simulations, which are a quasi-photographic visualization of unbuilt projects; this new digital visualization is able to create not only the illusion of reality but also the illusion of a photographic image.

The term *rendering* is commonly used to describe this form of computer-generated image. However, this description appears to be not quite appropriate since it refers in a narrow sense to the machine creation of a computer graphic from raw data. Thus the actual image is produced in a technical process. *Rendering* describes the pictorial output from a design model, which was created beforehand in an architectural design process, in a CAD program, the visualization itself not being the purpose of this process.[9] These types of images are certainly created from the base data of design programs, but this is done subsequently and with a specific intention that is not achievable using the design program itself. What is meant here are visualizations that have been designed for a specific purpose—for human vision—and that follow a specific logic. These images are certainly not representations of a given existing object—and are therefore extremely different from photography—but synthetic creations generated by digital means, designed views of unbuilt buildings. In a nutshell: on view is not built architecture, but architectural images.

The digital image in the design process

This architectural image is certainly part of what is described under the broad term of *architecture*, in exactly the same way as a hand drawing, a technically drawn plan, or a model—a tool, a medium, a form to keep and visualize data to advance the complex and many-handed process of creating a building.

The digitally created architectural image is omnipresent in today's architectural world. It may be a superficial conclusion, but it appears that architecture can no longer be considered by or communicated to the public without these images. Wherever architecture is discussed publicly, in the political debate on public buildings and urban design, as well as in advertisements and brochures in the private real estate market, there are digital image constructions of a similar kind: more or less realistic representations of unbuilt architecture.

On the other hand, the actual significance of the digital image for architectural practice, specifically here for the design process, is less simple to determine. Firstly, an architectural practice is a professional business operated by knowledgeable and experienced specialists. However, addressing a specific public, consumers, clients, or an institution managed by people who would be counted architecturally as laypersons has always been part of this business. Moreover, there is cause to suspect that design office practice has undergone a significant

141

Images for Consumption

10 A pioneering work is William J. Mitchell, *Computer-Aided Architectural Design*, New York 1977. For further reference, see Peter Zellner, *Hybrid Spaces: New Forms in Digital Architecture*, London 1999. On changing the design methodology, Rivka Oxman, "Theory and Design in the First Digital Age," in *Design Studies*, 27, 2006, 3 (May), pp. 229–65; Antoine Picon, *Digital Culture in Architecture: An Introduction for the Design Professionals*, Basel 2010; Mario Carpo (ed.), *The Digital Turn in Architecture* (AD Reader), Chichester 2013; Rivka Oxman and Robert Oxman (ed.), *Theories of the Digital in Architecture*, London 2014. The most comprehensive compendium is currently Ludger Hovestadt, Urs Hirschberg, and Oliver Fritz (ed.), *Atlas of Digital Architecture: Terminology, Concepts, Methods, Tools, Examples, Phenomena*, Basel 2020. Also Hubert Locher, "Atlas of Digital Architecture. Zur Rolle des digitalen Bildes in der Architektur—Ein Lesebericht," 4.10.2021 <https://www.digitalesbild.gwi.uni-muenchen.de/atlas-of-digital-architecture-zur-rolle-des-bildes-in-der-digitalen-architektur-ein-lesebericht/> (last accessed 19.1.2024).

11 Jörg H. Gleiter, Norbert Korrek, and Gerd Zimmermann (ed.), *Die Realität des Imaginären. Architektur und das digitale Bild*, 10. Internationales Bauhaus-Kolloquium Weimar 2007 (Schriften der Bauhaus-Universität Weimar, 120), Weimar 2008.

12 Sabine Ammon and Inge Hinterwaldner (ed.), *Bildlichkeit im Zeitalter der Modellierung. Operative Artefakte in Entwurfsprozessen der Architektur und des Ingenieurwesens*, Paderborn 2017.

13 Jörg H. Gleiter, "Vom Abreißen der Modellierungskette. Entwerfen im digitalen Zeitalter," in Ammon and Hinterwaldner, *Bildlichkeit im Zeitalter*, pp. 89–101.

14 Rivka Oxman, "Die Rolle des Bildes im digitalen Entwerfen. Bildprozessierung versus Prozessverbildlichung," in Ammon and Hinterwaldner, *Bildlichkeit im Zeitalter*, pp. 103–27, here pp. 104, 105.

15 Sabine Ammon, "Epilog. Vom Siegeszug der Bildlichkeit im Zeitalter der Modellierung," in Ammon and Hinterwaldner, *Bildlichkeit im Zeitalter*, pp. 399–426, here p. 399.

change in recent decades in that the design process itself can become pictorial, image-based, or be aiming to create a pictorial effect.

This subject—the imagery of the digital design—has only now been considered in detail in the academic discussion, which is surprising in view of the omnipresence of the phenomenon.[10] Standing out here is the anthology published by Jörg H. Gleiter, Norbert Korrek, and Gerd Zimmermann entitled *Realität des Imaginären. Architektur und das digitale Bild*, which emerged from an international colloquium attended by prominent speakers held at Bauhaus University Weimar in 2007.[11] In the introduction, Gerd Zimmermann highlights the part played by digital image technology in architecture. As he pointedly states, "architecture is principally image processing." In the age of digitality, however, the question of the power of the image comes up in new ways because, on the one hand, these digital images are always contrived, while, on the other, they can circulate globally and therefore be effective in completely new ways. Jörg H. Gleiter subsequently embeds this situation to some extent historically, referring to a number of stars of the postmodern—Aldo Rossi, James Stirling, Peter Eisenman, Oswald Mathias Ungers, and singling out their specific approaches to the image—to state that digital image technology, in the course of its extremely dynamic development, is now deeply inscribed into the body of architecture and will fundamentally change its nature.

These theses are confirmed and underpinned by the contributions in the 2017 anthology entitled *Bildlichkeit im Zeitalter der Modellierung* with reference to the design processes in architecture and engineering.[12] In several articles, the authors attempt to analyze the complex context of computer-based conceptual modeling and the image or pictorial realization that can actually be understood analytically only as systematic polarities. Jörg H. Gleiter describes "architectural design as a process of imaginative illustration and exemplary realization of architectural knowledge" that is the concatenation and interlacing of, on the one hand, modeling with the aim of an accurate "objectivization of the mere thought" (p. 92) and, on the other hand, imagery, which predominates at the beginning of every modeling process and for which, in contrast, a considerable "indeterminacy" is characteristic.[13] Rivka Oxman also considers this interlacing and speaks of a "new role of the image in generative design models" and determines it to be "a dominant agenda in both architectural theory and design practice."[14] Finally, in the epilogue, Sabine Ammon speaks of a "triumphal procession of imagery." The "use of computer-based models" has, according to her conclusion, "not held back the significance of image-based methods." On the contrary, the possibilities of computer-based architectural design have produced "new forms of image use" and not displaced the old in any way.[15]

Emerging from the overall tenor of the cursory list of literature presented here is the view that the new digital tools and methods have enriched architectural design practice with a completely new pictorial dimension. The more recent generation of design programs combines visual and computer processes. A wide spectrum of types of visualizations function at different phases of the design to provide representations of complex information that are "legible to humans." In principle, it can also be said that, where necessary, designing has become a three-dimensional process: "the computer enables the designer to play games

142

Hubert Locher

16 Bernhard Langer, "Computer-darstellung. Vom Programm zum digitalen Ökosystem," in *Die Medien der Architektur*, ed. Wolfgang Sonne, Munich 2011, pp. 157–68, here p. 163.

17 Marco Hemmerling emphasizes this in "3D Modelling," in Hovestadt, Hirschberg, and Fritz, *Atlas of Digital Architecture*, pp. 59–90, here p. 60, in comparison with the sculptor: "With 3D modelling, the architect or designer, like a sculptor, makes decisions that are informed by the design process itself: a sculptor shapes its object—either by chipping away at it or by bending, molding, adding to [...] and at any and every point is able to review the steps just taken and, based on these, consider the next ones. [...] 3D modelling allows us as architect to do the same."

18 See the contribution from Dominik Lengyel and Catherine Toulouse, pp. 10–19.

19 See → Image 36, p. 106. On the problem of signature architecture, see Nadja Alaily-Mattar, Davide Ponzini, and Alain Thierstein (ed.), *About Star Architecture: Reflecting on Cities in Europe*, Cham 2020.

of 'what would happen if': a scenario based on certain parameters is simulated in order to then check 'in real time' what changes [occur] when certain parameters are manipulated. [...] Architecture is no longer conceived through planimetric representations (the plan is no longer *le générateur*), but is seen more as a framework of three-dimensional structures that are formed in a simulated environment by the hand (or the mouse) of the architect [...]."[16] Without doubt, digital design tools offer increasing possibilities to achieve results using computed (algorithmic) data. However, at the same time, there is the opportunity to create the object formed during the design process continuously and three-dimensionally on digital models displayed on the computer monitor.[17] How the process described here—the increasingly powerful growing imagery gained by architectural design, at least potentially, from the use of digital technology: architectural design becoming artistic design—works on the general understanding is difficult to gauge. Whether and to what extent the visual appearance of a planned building already in the process of design is enhanced by this depends also on the type of project and the choice of design approach.[18]

If consideration of the architectural process is widened enough and looks beyond the work involved in the design to include the previous and assimilated contexts, the people involved, in other words the client, the competitive environment, the possibilities of performative presentation, and above all the public, the consumers, it can be said with certainty that, thanks to the new possibilities of digital image generation, visualization has clearly gained importance, and with that in particular the illusionistic, quasi-photographic realistic type.

Architecture is integrated into a media context more strongly than ever before. In the early stages, a design must be communicated through media, principally asserting and making the case for itself in the form of an image. In retrospect or even during the building process, the convincing power of visual presentation plays a central role—for example in the marketing of residential properties that are to be adjusted or fitted out to suit a customer's wishes. Continual promotion is crucial for the success of public buildings, as was the case for the Hamburg Elbphilharmonie designed by Herzog & de Meuron, which became a signature building for the Hanseatic city even before it had been completed.[19] It could be safely assumed that the visualizations produced highlighted the objective that was still to be achieved in the realization at that time. What comes into play here is that the digital architectural image created in the course of the design process is a visual promise for the future. This image generated by the computer on the basis of appropriate design data is able literally to be a vision. Appearing as a first realization of an architectural construct, it takes on a critical form—decisive for success, for the chances of realizing a design as a building in the non-virtual world—and is a means of inviting its realization.

The image as the interface with the public

Even if, in a certain sense, such images bear the underlying burden of overexpectation, images have always been designed for this very situation: an image always shows only a view and not the thing itself; it is

143

Images for Consumption

20 See the contribution from Florian Henrich, pp. 20–33.

21 Herbert Kiefer, "Renderverbot. Wie man im Saarland die Chancengleichheit bei Wettbewerben erhöhen will," in *Bauwelt*, 101, 2010, 11 (12 Mar.), pp. 12–13.

22 Ibid., p. 13.

23 Ibid.

24 Klaus D. Nielen, *Immobilien-Marketing. Vermarktung von Bauträgermaßnahmen und Bestands-Immobilien (Teil 1)*, Düsseldorf 1996. Extracts from this book also appear in 1997 as an eleven-part "Nielen-Marketingserie" in *Immobilien-Zeitung*.

the nature of the image that its material appearance only stimulates the observer's power of imagination. Unlike a picture in the familiar adage, it does not paint a thousand words; it suggests to the viewers that they formulate these words themselves. The actual image arises only in the course of its reception as an idea. Misuse, the image distracting from the important, is a legitimate fear. The image is therefore also dangerous because it could easily be confused with the actual thing to which it is supposed only to refer, wherein lies also an opportunity.

The mistrust of the image, which can be traced back to the philosophy of Plato, is present at widely varying degrees in different times and contexts. However, it is particularly pronounced in modern architecture. Postmodern strategies intervene precisely at this point and instigate a modern iconoclastic controversy. However, as a result, the attitudes soften toward the end of the twentieth century, on the one hand as a result of the omnipresence of the image in the new media worlds, and on the other because of the speed of adoption of digital visualization technologies in architectural practice, which leads to the image and imagery both becoming integrated into the process of architectural design. The convoluted trail of this process, which takes place over a good three decades, can be accurately traced in the specialist journals.[20] In doing so, a skepticism of images again emerges. Just one example of this is provided by an article in *Bauwelt* during 2010, which reports that a "rendering ban" is imposed by the rules for a competition.[21] In the view of the article's author, renderings, by which are meant digitally created perspective visualizations, are not necessary and possibly even misleading for the evaluation of architectural projects by the jury members. Such images are "'too costly, too eye-catching, too subjective.'"[22] The tone of this arbitrarily selected article is typical, insofar as its author firmly believes it will receive general approval, as it is simply about being fair and fending off cheats; a competition should be decided on the basis of "objective and comprehensible criteria."[23]

The second argument is connected with this mistrust of the truthfulness of the image and is equally important, even though it is seldom discussed in the specialist journals: illusionistic, perspective visualizations do not represent the way experts, the people producing the architecture, view the design, but rather how the layperson sees it. They play to the gallery, to the public; they are intended for marketing. A look in a typical guide on real estate marketing from 1996, the year from which the digital turning point becomes noticeable, may serve as an illustration.[24] One of the main chapters is exclusively concerned with the "presentation of the real estate portfolio," which is primarily about achieving success through the sales brochure. Its author, Klaus D. Nielen, a marketing specialist and publisher of several books on the subject, bestows special importance on the image according to the principle that real estate is only as good as how it appears "in the eyes of the potential purchasers," because buying real estate is an "emotional act with a rational alibi" in general (p. 135). The image must also speak to the ideas already held by the potential purchasers. Although the recommendations on this are certainly rather trivial, nevertheless they are very revealing: because the prospective purchasers as laypersons would be overburdened by "over-technical representations," a quasi-natural image is required to give a view closer to that of an onlooker's real perspective. Artistic

144

Hubert Locher

25 In 1995, *Immobilien-Zeitung* discussed the possibility of computer and video simulations with the cost of a photorealistic freeze-frame put at 18,000 to 25,000 Deutschmarks. Gerhard Saß, "Computergestützte Architektursimulation als Marketing-Instrument der Immobilienwirtschaft," in *Immobilien-Zeitung* 1995, 27.7.1995, No. 16, p. 9 <https://www.iz.de/unternehmen/news/-computergestuet-architektur-simulat-als-market-instrum-der-immobilienwirtsch-von-der-fotorealistisc-wiederg-bis-zum-wal-thro-all-istmoegl--ein-beit-von-2559> (last accessed 19.1.2024).

26 Nielen, *Immobilien-Marketing*, p. 185: "Therefore you should guard against incorporating excessively modern style elements into your building representations, even though they might have artistic value."

27 Friederike Meyer in conversation with Justus Ettemeyer of EVE images, in *Bauwelt*, 107, 2016, 33 (26 Aug.), pp. 22–25, here p. 22.

28 Friederike Meyer in conversation with Christoph Reichen and Malte Kloes from bildbau, in *Bauwelt*, 107, 2016, 33 (26 Aug.), pp. 26–29, here p. 26.

stylizations in which the hand and the imagination of a designer have obviously been involved are to be avoided. The ideal visualization needs to be rich in detail and preferably in color: "The color representation beats black and white, provided that the color representation comes very close or exceeds it in terms of reality!" (p. 175) Now here lies the potential of the increasingly popular "computer simulation," which the author is sure will shape the future of the real estate industry by the creation of "sales-motivating property portfolios" (p. 177), because the objective can be more easily achieved with their help: a natural-looking, photorealistic representation.[25] Explicitly—and here lies the difference from any possible photograph—it should not depict any form of present situation; the "task of building representation" is much more "the anticipation of a future perspective" (p. 180). However, this is not concerned with the idea of the seller or even the design intention of the architect (p. 169). The sole measure for the "correctness of the representation" is the fulfillment of the expectations of the potential purchaser.[26]

The possibilities of the developments associated with digitally generated "near-realistic" visualizations over the following years are not without significance for those producing them. Even in the journal *Bauwelt*, which is aimed at the creators of architecture and not the real estate industry, realistic-looking visualizations are discussed as a necessary marketing tool that can be crucial to success also in competitions, albeit not until twenty years later, and are even considered to be of possible relevance for the design. The ambivalence can already be seen in 2016 in the title of issue 33. "Ungebautes inszenieren—Architektur verkaufen" (Staging the unbuilt—selling architecture). Various articles give more details about the situation and define the specific business field of visualization, while differentiating it from architectural design. In the interview, Justus Ettemeyer from EVE images ("one of the largest rendering firms in Europe") points out that investors not architects are his main customers and emphasizes that his company does not make architecture, it makes images. "We make images. Architects design."[27] The "competition rendering" is "more illustrative, more graphical," and can "tell a story"; whereas "sales images" "communicate a perception of life. Sun, shadow, and beautiful colors dominate" (p. 23) in the photorealistic mode. "Rendering is the same as photographing for me. It doesn't matter whether you create an image digitally or with a camera by photography" (p. 24).

In the same issue of *Bauwelt*, Malte Kloes and Christoph Reichen from the Swiss company bildbau GmbH emphasize the potential significance of visualization, including for design. Many architects "believe in understanding everything in plans and do not need images."[28] However, in the architectural office, it is often said that visualization leads to overthinking of the design. Although, unfortunately, they are involved "mostly toward the end" (p. 26), the pair see themselves as members of the design team. Their contribution consists in clarifying the aesthetic effect. It is basically about questions of stylistics, the representation, which must correspond with the mood of the architecture: the degree of detail of the image, the level of abstraction, the light mood, and the question of color are agreed in dialogue with the architects doing the design. These components of the visualization need to be finely tuned

145

Images for Consumption

29 See <https://www.maltekloes.ch/#projekte> and <https://wallimannreichen.ch/> (last accessed 19.1.2024).

30 See Florian Henrich, "Die Diskussion des digitalen Bildes in den Architekturzeitschriften," in *Rendering / Visualisierung* (Begriffe des digitalen Bildes, 5), ed. Hubert Locher, Dominik Lengyel, Florian Henrich, and Catherine Toulouse, Munich 2024, pp. 28–54. DOI: https://doi.org/10.5282/ubm.epub.109218

31 Advertisement by Herzog & de Meuron in *Bauwelt*, 98, 2007, 25 (1 July), p. 44, top right.

in order to avoid creating overdramatic illustrations instead of the "good images" that result "from realistic materiality and light mood" (p. 29).

What is touched upon in the quoted articles and comes up increasingly frequently in discussions is the fear of misleading, exaggerated visualization, of images "that over-stage" the subject (p. 26). What can lead to misunderstandings and possibly complaints in the field of marketing or can be averted in advance by a reference to the illustration-like nature of the presentations can be disadvantageous in competitions if an excessive degree of detail has a distracting or intrusive effect; the jury—normally a committee of architectural specialists—does not wish to be importuned by rhetorical images.

The competition or sales perspective is in itself only one of many fields of application of architectural visualization. Self-promotion using architectural images by the architectural office involved is of great importance as well. The architect's website has become a digital showcase in which, independent of or in advance of a possible commissioning, the self-image and attitude of an office are presented on the basis of its designed and completed projects. In general, has competence in visualization gained in importance, or is it competence in handling the stylistic parameters of architectural appearance as components of the design?

Whatever the case, the visualization specialists at bildbau have changed sides since 2019 and now run their own design office. Malte Kloes and Christoph Estrada Reichen together with Nicole Maria Wallimann[29] scintillate today with simple yet elegant websites that present their projects by means of virtuoso renderings. Above all, Wallimann / Reichen Architekten offers the almost text-free, illusionistic image containing sporadic "narrative" elements as a means of access. In every case, however, the information is stylized in a characteristic way encapsulating the aesthetic attitude of the office.

Questions of "style"—the aesthetic of the digital image in use

During the period studied, a continuous development in the sense of an increasing differentiation, which could possibly be termed a consciousness of style, becomes apparent. The power of the image gains recognition. The architectural office needs a pictorial language characteristic of its self-image for its visual presentations. This requires specialist skills. Architectural experience is a prerequisite, but success in this respect calls for expertise in working with the digital image. Job advertisements also differentiate between the relevant fields of activity.[30] The prominent Swiss architectural practice Herzog & de Meuron—which sets the standard in many respects by its use of the architectural image and imagery in architecture—searches in an advertisement in *Bauwelt* 2007, issue 25 for an "Architectural Imagemaker," who is described as follows: "You create images that communicate, over and above conveying the spatial and architectural context, a visual impression of the principle of the concept and the sought-after atmosphere. You are conscious that atmospheric pictorial language is the key to visual communication."[31] These sentences say that there is a fundamental difference between design and visualization, but both aim to convey "atmosphere." The

146

Hubert Locher

32 Refer to an attempt at reconciliation by Gernot Böhme, "Atmosphären als Gegenstand der Architektur," in *Herzog & de Meuron. Naturgeschichte*, ed. Philip Ursprung, exhib. cat. Canadian Centre for Architecture, Baden (CH) 2002, pp. 410–17, here p. 414. Emphasis in original.

33 "Über Architektur und Bild. Jacques Herzog and Gottfried Boehm im Gespräch," on August 18, 2004, on the occasion of the exhibition "Herzog & de Meuron: No. 250. Eine Ausstellung" at the Schaulager Basel <https://www.herzogdemeuron.com/writings/uber-architektur-und-bild/> (last accessed 19.1.2024).

implication is that the design aims for "atmosphere," while at the same time speaking of a "pictorial language" that itself is "atmospheric."

What is meant by that? It is a mood, a sensual appeal, emanating from an object; in the literal sense it would be what surrounds a thing and determines its appearance and special sensory effect. To what extent, however, can such a mood be ascribed to the object? Is the mood not largely determined by variations in the circumstances, the light, the weather? That would certainly apply. However, atmosphere is above all something that takes the form of a human emotion. The philosopher Gernot Böhme in relation to architecture—and here particularly with respect to the buildings of Herzog & de Meuron—spoke of a "sense" of the character of a space that currently surrounds us and which we can access physically and spatially: "We sense what sort of a space surrounds us. We sense its atmosphere."[32] In other words, it would not be so much about what is seen; and yet the medium of the image is obviously suitable to bring this "sense" alive through seeing even in the absence of an accessible building.

This would be precisely the task of architectural visualization if "atmospheric quality" is regarded as an important characteristic of good architecture. Herzog & de Meuron claims this for its work. It is, however, generally a principal aspect, a characteristic of any architectural culture developed over the last few decades in a deliberate move away from postmodern pictoriality: an architecture that cannot be called pictorial in the sense of a communicative symbol but which addresses and targets much more the imagination of the viewer in order to evoke a flash of imagination. Herzog & de Meuron have this to say on the issue: "In the end, we are interested in the possibilities of triggering the potential of the image in those perceiving it."[33] The role of architectural visualization in such a conception is to pictorially anticipate this postulated aesthetic potential of the future building in a simulation.

A look at the examples and development of the digital architectural representation shows this claim to be a vision, an ideal achievable to a greater or lesser extent. These types of images can initially provide nothing other than a convincing three-dimensional illusion. The model is in principle a view that communicates three-dimensionality, a perspective dependent on the chosen viewing point. However, this view must be supplemented by what lies in between, by the "air," by precisely the "atmosphere," which is actually invisible but determines the appearance. The digital architectural image therefore requires compositional modifications of the model view, which could be described as stylizations. They affect the whole image in the form of "filters." This stylistic nuance, as it also could be described, combines with the addition of representational subjects that are not part of the architecture. The most powerful means of creating an atmosphere is, however, the allusion, the hint at previous images, presentations, topoi that are called upon or implied. They are all genuine artistic, even fine-art, processes, which are given a technically induced application in the digital architectural image.

The wide range of uses can be seen in the examples in this book. The three chosen to be discussed here are suitable for highlighting the solution of specific problems of visualization in relation to the communicative function of these images. The communicative function is the

147

Images for Consumption

34 Roland Barthes, "L'effet de réel," in *Communications*, 1968, 11 (Mar.), pp. 81–90.

primary consideration because the architectural image is the crucial interface; it must act on the imagination of the consumers, the public. However, the effect should be more than stimulation; it should win over and convince them.

One of the ways this can be done is by integrating the new into the familiar in a landscape, a known situation. The design for a department store at a prominent location in Innsbruck provides a perfect example (→ Image 34). The image places the new building into the existing context, making it an element of the developing urban environment. A car and a random street sign create the *"effet de réel"* in precisely the way Roland Barthes described this idea in literature.[34] The actual subject, a facade designed in extreme contrast to its surroundings, is almost made to disappear in the perspective. This is the aim, because there is an intense public debate about the disfigurement of this "heavenly city," which has always understood urbanity in relation to its Alpine setting. The design was not successful, but the image strategy is nevertheless highly effective.

What atmosphere involves can best be understood in relation to the effects of the light, the lighting. Light structures the continuous space; however, it can also set accents. Light has always been a means of creating "mood." As with the visualization of the previously mentioned Hamburg Elbphilharmonie by Herzog & de Meuron, one of the most striking "iconic" architectural projects of recent decades, the night image is particularly effective (→ Image 36). The representation carries with it a historical allusion to Bruno Taut's Stadtkrone, or City Crown, which is certainly a source of inspiration, but here it is all about the light effect, which succeeds in emphasizing the elementary contrast of a dark plinth and the incised, perforated superstructure, revealing itself in the light effects, the main motif of the tower projecting upward from the water—a structure that gives people a place, a "space-ship," an ark, reaching for the heavens.

In contrast to a design staging as a city crown illuminated against the night, C.F. Møller Architects decided to set the design in an evening light mood (→ Image 47) in the 2017 competition for a new campus at the Via University College in Horsens, Denmark. The visualization relies on light as a symbol for pulsating student life on the future campus. This image intention extends so far that the structures and the details of the buildings are almost hidden and even darkened. The mood-setting qualities of the materials are subdued and hardly recognizable. The project was built. The C.F. Møller Architects website shows comprehensive documentation of the actual building, with descriptions, a photo gallery, diagrams, site studies, layouts, drawings, and sketches. The building and the website achieve what initially could only be promised in the digital representation. However, the competition visualization does not appear in the project presentation. It has been replaced by the actual photograph.

Hubert Locher

35 Cf. Olivier Meystre, "Hand in Hand: analog und digital," in *Bauwelt*, 108, 2017, 24 (1 Dec.), pp. 60–63.

Digital by hand

Does photography finally beat the digital image after all? It is impossible to generalize. The individual case of the last example, however, may indicate that the fictional image is still mistrusted, or that the photograph is considered more expressive, more reputable. The possibility of direct comparison is at least avoided—reality is not to be measured against architectural fiction. The atmospheric architectural image, the design of which using digital tools has become a profession in its own right, without which architecture would be inconceivable in its modern form, is still regarded by the designing architects as a "medium," a means of communication. The effect of an illusion is required, but the digital image is still only a means to an end. As was made clear earlier, rendering and photography are ultimately not played off against one another, because they fulfill two different functions. Rendering is used because the design cannot yet be photographed in its built state. All the more interesting, then, that there is obviously a widespread need, even within architectural circles, to have the design appear like a photograph of the realized building and at the same time create a staging for it with the appropriate atmosphere. Rendering should not only be seen as a derivative of photography, but also as a specific and malleable image quality.

It can therefore be observed that today the architectural representation is actively pressing ahead with the drive to embrace digital technologies, that its results are perfectly designed and orchestrated—as the websites of the architectural offices mentioned here, from GRAFT Architekten to C.F. Møller Architects, impressively prove. Digital technology is essential in this context and is for the most part staged as such. However, architecture desires to continue to be at least potentially an artistic profession—design according to human imagination. and in this sense analog, so to speak. This is shown not least in recent times by an increasingly observed tendency of digital architectural visualization to distance itself from conventional illusionistic rendering and move in the direction of a much more graphic, abstract form of representation—albeit using digital means.[35]

149

Hubert Locher,
Florian Henrich

The Dialectic of the Digital Image in the Architectural Process

In our research project "Architecture Transformed—Architectural Processes in the Digital Image Space," we looked into the question of the extent to which the digital image has changed the design and visualization of architecture. The starting point is the assumption that visual representation as well as the accompanying media transformations are generally integral components of architecture. The production and the way in which architecture is presented and understood are largely determined by the media used for their depiction. Digitalization has led to equally profound changes on the level of both the design and the visual presentation of architecture, examples of which were studied as part of the project. The guiding idea was therefore the question of how much use is made of the digital image today in the architectural process, how the digital image affects architecture, and to what extent we can now speak of "digital architecture."

In order to make the fundamental change from the analog to the digital architectural image tangible and generally gain a clear idea of the digital architectural image, we approached the phenomenon from two sides: while the Cottbus subproject considered digital image production from the *point of view of architecture practice* and analyzed the digital image as an elemental component of digital design and visualization tools in their effects on the created results, the Marburg side of the project focused on conducting an *analytic historical* reconstruction of the genesis of digital architectural representation, its media diffusion and reception, as well as determining the aesthetic features of the digital architectural image and the criticism of its application as a means of communication. In this way, design and visualization were linked with one another, and production and representation of architecture considered in their context.

This shows that there is a principal difference between the methods of visual representation of architecture in the context of design and designing on the one hand, and in the context of visualizing, rendering, and representative depiction or communicative purposes on the other. The digital image can be conceived both as something processual, a direct interface that feeds back into and influences the iterative process of design, and as a presentation image, as the result and product of a design process focused on visual demonstration. While both instances are concerned with visual representations, they differ fundamentally in their appearance, function, and application. The digital image as part of architectural design tools, as a visual component of the digital tool, is different. It requires a different form of imagery from the digital image used in representative design visualization. Architectural design and visualization represent two different processes, in which distinguishable modes of imagery are employed and various types of digital images generated.

It became clear in the course of our investigation that, where the two spheres of processual design and subsequent visualization relate to one another in a natural way, the extremely dynamic development of the available digital methods over recent decades has led to an increased penetration and an intensified interrelationship. The field of design has generally seen an increasing importance accorded to visualization, to pictorial, vivid representations, as is evidenced by the example of the Design Technologies Department in the offices of Herzog & de Meuron:

151

1   Anh-Linh Ngo and Alexandra Nehmer in conversation with Steffen Riegas and Michael Drobnik (HdeM), "Komplexitäts-management," in *ARCH+*, 2018, 233 (Nov.), pp. 80–87, here p. 82.

2   Cf. Hubert Locher, "Atlas of Digital Architecture. Zur Rolle des Bildes in der digitalen Architektur—Ein Lesebericht," 4.10.2021 <https://www.digi-talesbild.gwi.uni-muenchen.de/atlas-of-digital-architecture-zur-rolle-des-bildes-in-der-digitalen-architektur-ein-lesebericht/> (last accessed 17.1.2024).

3   See the contribution from Dominik Lengyel and Catherine Toulouse, pp. 10–19.

"With complex buildings, four sections are enough to show the intention, but it is quite something else to be able to check every specific situation in and around the building based on a model. Visualizing these situations has become more and more like a working tool that helps us in making decisions. [...] Visualizations have become tools in themselves, not least because of the increasing possibilities and importance of virtual reality and real-time rendering. Today, the focus of the visualization team is much more on software use and programming."[1]

In view of this noticeable current development of increasingly frequent combinations of design and visualization, architecture appears today, in the digital age, as profoundly shaped by digital imagery. A proposed building can be checked for its visual effect, appropriately conceived and designed in practically all phases of the design, more or less from the beginning using current digital design programs. In this way, the image becomes both the means of verification and a record of the ideals to be achieved, which form the basis of a design prior to any kind of decision to build being made. This means not only those lavishly designed, suggestive presentation images produced outside the design process and intended to communicate and market the design to the outside world as in the pre-digital age, which may be commonly referred to as renderings but are in no way simple to produce as part of a purely technical process. The decisive factor in the fusion of design and visualization seems to lie rather more in the growing importance of elementary visuality for the design process itself. The pictorial representation in the form of a two-dimensional view materialized virtually on the computer monitor or subsequently on paper as a print occupies a new role as a digitally modeled pictorial impression that can be called up with little time and effort in as many phases of the design as necessary during the iterative process of its improvement. Accordingly, with reference to the use of digital design and visualization tools, architecture is thought and conceived more strongly than ever to "start from the image."[2] Of course, this is also due to those representative digital image products, communicating the design in a suggestive, persuasive, and fashionable way to the outside world in the form of circulating media artifacts and as such indirectly affecting the design process and the people involved in it.

The image as part of the tool

As the practical analysis in the Cottbus subproject shows, ever more imagery is used when designing in a digital environment. The possibilities of the expansion of its use, and also the limits for its use in the design, depend greatly on the type of design software chosen.[3] The computer enables a continuous, "fluid,"[4] free design process, no longer separated into plan, elevation, and section, but in the perspective view. The design represented virtually on the two-dimensional computer monitor screen can be designed to a certain extent artistically as a three-dimensional figure; in other words, it is modeled as an "image" with the view as its starting point.

152

Hubert Locher, Florian Henrich

4   Cf. Sophie Ramm, "Fluide Architektur," in *Fluidität*, ed. Hanni Geiger and Julian Stalter (Begriffe des digitalen Bildes, 4), Munich 2023, pp. 50–67, here p. 56. DOI: https://doi.org/10.5282/ubm/epub.105066

5   Wassili Luckhardt, "Vom Entwerfen," in *Stadtbaukunst alter und neuer Zeit*, 2, 1921, 11 (1 Sept.), pp. 169–70, here p. 170.

6   Inge Hinterwaldner, "Prolog. Modellhaftigkeit und Bildlichkeit in Entwurfsartefakten," in *Bildlichkeit im Zeitalter der Modellierung. Operative Artefakte in Entwurfsprozessen der Architektur und des Ingenieurwesens*, ed. Sabine Ammon and Inge Hinterwaldner, Munich 2017, pp. 13–30, here p. 14. Emphasis in original.

7   Cf. Svenia Schneider, *Blob-Architektur für das 21. Jahrhundert. Neues Paradigma oder Relaunch einer ehrwürdigen Tradition?*, Marburg 2012; Carin M. Schirmacher, *Paradoxien des Digital Turn in der Architektur 1990–2015. Von den Verlockungen des Organischen: digitales Entwerfen zwischen informellem Denken und biomorphem Resultat*, Berlin 2018.

8   See Barbara Wittmann, *Werkzeuge des Entwerfens*, Zürich 2018.

Intuitive three-dimensional design is certainly not a genuinely digital phenomenon. In 1921, Wassili Luckhardt mentioned a means "that is as old as time"—clay modeling: "One places the pencil and ruler to one side, takes the clay or plasticine and begins to knead it, starting from scratch, without warning or outside influence."[5] (Fig. 1) What is much more revealing is that this approach to design was successfully transferred to the computer and relocated in virtual space. That this digital image space ends up being two-dimensional due to the restrictions of its reproduction on the computer monitor does not present a contradiction, even if an architectural model in everyday terms is normally understood to be a material, three-dimensional, sculptural object. In the field of digital design, the practitioners generally speak "of a computer *model* as being an *image* observed on a computer monitor."[6]

Also significant in this context is the formal similarity between Luckhardt's presented design, which could be described as a dynamic "blob" with a jagged city crown, and the computer-generated designs and buildings of a Greg Lynn or UNStudio. This striking parallelism of shape[7] could, on the one hand, be seen as indicating the success of three-dimensional design using the computer. Free-form designs, like those developed three-dimensionally by hand in Luckhardt's time, are now possible on the computer monitor and can be technically implemented with the help of digital design tools. On the other hand, the similarity of computer-aided architectural designs to supposed predecessors from the pre-digital age could equally indicate that "digital architecture" forms owe primarily nothing to digital design tools, as was repeatedly postulated by various sides during the digitalization of architectural practice and is still sometimes heard today.

That is evident in the examples from practice. Like all the other tools, the digital design tool expands and limits the scope of possibilities in the architectural design process in its own specific ways.[8] Thus a city such as Leipzig has a multitude of buildings that practically form their own type based on their design repertoire and construction during the 1990s, not infrequently described in a derogatory way as "commercial architecture" or "post-unification architecture." (Fig. 2) What appears as a style is also conditioned by the shaping qualities or standardizing effects of using CAD software, with its preference for simple geometric basic forms such as the cube or cylinder.

As the Cottbus study shows, however, these are design solutions that are not set in advance by the digital design tool used; they originate from the users. A pronounced boom of tall, rectangular, more or less rhythmically gridded facades that are also occasionally described disparagingly as "barcode" architecture has been apparent for a long time in current architectural practice, as a reaction to the stand-alone blob icons with their complex and highly individual shapes. Here as well, the computer is an essential element in the design process, although this is not necessarily apparent at first glance from the constructed shape (Fig. 3). While the "blob" has obviously shown that complex architectural forms can not only be invented with the computer but also be made technically realizable, in contrast to the subsequent development in the direction of "barcode," it is also apparent that the use of the computer in the design process is in no way bound to lead to a specific shape, to

153

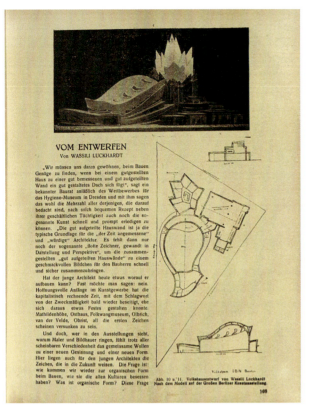

Fig. 1, Wassili Luckhardt, "Vom Entwerfen," in *Stadtbaukunst alter und neuer Zeit*, 1921, issue 11, p. 169

Fig. 2, Leipzig post-unification "commercial architecture," photographs: © Florian Henrich

Fig. 3, Architekturbüro Ratschko, Meininger Hotel Bremen (during construction), spring 2022, photograph: © Florian Henrich

9   Oskar Graf, "Die Statik, die Konstruktion und der Dekonstruktivismus," in *Bauwelt*, 80, 1989, 26 (7 July), p. 1260.

10 Ulf Meyer, "Das Imperium schlägt zurück. CAD und die Formfindung der Sporthalle in Halstenbek," in *Bauwelt*, 88, 1997, 45 (28 Nov.), pp. 2524–27, here p. 2525.

11 Boris Schade-Büsow in conversation with Norbert Palz and Matthias Castorph, "Werkzeug, Revolution und Evolution," in *Bauwelt*, 102, 2011, 23 (10 June), pp. 17–21, here p. 17.

12 Peter Kulka and Ulrich Königs, "Sportstadion Chemnitz 2002," in *Bauwelt*, 87, 1996, 12 (29 Mar.), pp. 728–33, here p. 729.

13 Werner Haker, "Architektur im Computer," in *Werk, Bauen+Wohnen*, 76, 1989, 3, pp. 52–58, here p. 56.

a specific architectural result that emerges literally automatically from the digital design tools.

Even in "digital architecture," as already in the "functionalism" of the modern, a form is not passively "found" in a technical process, it is designed in a more or less complex, multi-phase, iterative process. As the "blob" makes clear, formal complexity is seen as almost a central feature of "digital architecture." As has already been seen in the case of deconstructivist architectural projects of the 1980s and '90s, the computer is a prerequisite for breaking the rules, logic, and rationalism of built structures through appropriate design calculations and structural analyses, "but at great cost and effort."[9] With the "blob," it was undeniably the case that not only the construction but also the building shapes are so complex that they "are manageable only on the computer."[10] Quite a number of the components used in these buildings are unique and have to be individually manufactured using digital processes.

In this case, the computer does not lead to an increase in rationality and simplification, which could have been reasonably expected, but allows mastery of increased complexity on the levels of design, construction, and logistics, a complexity that it alone has made possible. Formal complexity becomes a visible sign of the technical avant-garde in a self-perpetuating, increasing spiral of technological advances and complexity of forms. In this respect, it is about buildings such as the Stuttgart Mercedes-Benz Museum by UNStudio (2001–6) or the Beijing National Stadium by Herzog & de Meuron (2002–8), which are iconic "solitaires radiating a certain autism."[11] However, this refers above all to the literally spectacular, those buildings designed for visual effect, virtuoso proofs of performance for technological progressiveness, in which the complexity is increased to demonstrate technical feasibility, while all the time probing, maximizing the possible, and expanding its boundaries.

A crucial aspect is that, even in the digital age, designers often have "a specific effect in their mind's eye that then has to be created with an appropriate form of building."[12] Whether the design idea takes a tangible form only during the visually constituted, image-heavy digital design process or existed beforehand, the process of digital form-finding is, in the end, an architectural act of form-giving. As it is possible to create not only "blob" or "barcode" but also in principle any conceivable form of architecture using the computer, this form is always the result of the people who work with the digital design tools, and thus always the result of a more or less conscious aesthetic decision.

The fundamental openness or universality of the digital design tool in relation to form has already been critically assessed in terms of its consequences for architecture, and, significantly, a direct link to the increasing importance of imagery in digital design was established. According to Werner Haker in 1989:

> "It was never so easy to create images during architectural design, and it was never as quick and precise to produce detailed drawings as with CAD. [...] The corset of the right angle has become obsolete, and the wildest polygamies and curve orgies can playfully, yes only too playfully, be measured. [...] It was never so easy, so quick to design nonsense."[13]

155

The Dialectic of the Digital Image in the Architectural Process

14 Greg Lynn, "Das Gefaltete, das Biegsame und das Geschmeidige," in *ARCH+*, 1996, 131 (April), pp. 62–65, here p. 65.

15 Patrik Schumacher, "Parametrismus. Der neue International Style," in *ARCH+*, 2009, 195 (Nov.), pp. 106–13, here p. 107.

16 Wolfgang Wagener, "Die Morphologie des Formlosen," in *ARCH+*, 1997, 138 (Oct.), pp. 82–85, here p. 83.

17 Nikolaus Kuhnert and Angelika Schnell, "Von der Box zum Blob und wieder zurück," in *ARCH+*, 1999, 148 (Oct.), pp. 20–21, here p. 20.

18 Florian Böhm, "Neue Dimensionen für die Architektur?," in *ARCH+*, 1999, 148 (Oct.), pp. 103–5, here p. 105.

19 Sabine Kraft and Schirin Taraz-Breinholt, "Zu diesem Heft," in *ARCH+*, 2002, 159/160 (May), p. 20.

20 Sabine Kraft, "Anpassungen," in *ARCH+*, 2008, 188 (July), p. 4.

Against this background, argumentative strivings to objectify designers' own activities appear in the journals from the mid-1990s, while the criticism endeavors to expose them as the legitimization rhetoric for preferences of form. It is nothing less than the reproach of "formalism," which has been ever present in the discussion of architecture since the beginning of the modern. In 1996, for example, Greg Lynn points out that the "formal affinities" of his designs "react to eventualities," "beyond formalism in a world of outside influences."[14] In 2009, Patrik Schumacher elevates "parametricism" even more, to a "new international style," a digital phenomenon of global validity, that makes "postmodern and deconstructivism" into "transitional episodes."[15] In contrast to this, it had been postulated ten years earlier that the "biological approach to form-finding [...] in architecture had become a style that has appeared only recently in projects around the world. [...] 'Blobs' are the current language of form."[16] Similarly subject to criticism is the view that these images are considered as "generated on the computer and [...] therefore a purely geometric and hence rationalized form,"[17] because it is assumed that through this postulate "a seeming rationality of architecture would be symbolized" to a much greater extent. Therefore, the "recourse to geometry" could be seen "as only a metaphorical foundation."[18] This "does not explain how the form gets into the designer's mind or comes out of the computer."[19] It is, however, an error to assume that the architectural design would emerge full-blown from the digital design tools alone,

"in which the computer with the help of genetic algorithms evolves random forms, their choice being determined by pseudo-rational evaluation criteria or arbitrary freezing of the process ... and the necessary army of specialists and technicians required for their materialization."[20]

The image as a representative medium

Along with the majority of the journal authors who were contacted during the course of the research for the project, we looked at the assumption of determinism of form by the digital tool rather skeptically. Like every tool, design software of whatever genre enables new forms or suggests them to designers, and offers great heuristic potential for the architectural design process, without that software specifying or predetermining those sorts of architectural solutions.

We therefore speak about a media shaping not only of architecture, concept and idea, but also of the design process and, with that, the built form through the digital image, the shaping we regard as feedback on the design from the received images as part of a dialectic process. The media-specific shaping of what architecture is happens not only through the image as a visual component of the digital design tools but also through the image as a specific type of representation. Realized architecture is, if it is not visited and experienced, dependent on media to communicate it through its pictorial representation, in exactly the same way as the design. Unlike the physical building, the representation of which, with all the unavoidable distortions or deliberate, calculated

Hubert Locher, Florian Henrich

21 Cf. for the photography: Hubert Locher and Rolf Sachsse (ed.), *Architektur Fotografie. Darstellung—Verwendung—Gestaltung*, Berlin and Munich 2016.

22 See the contribution from Hubert Locher, pp. 138–149.

23 See the contribution from Florian Henrich, pp. 20–33, and Florian Henrich, "Die Diskussion des digitalen Bildes in den Architekturzeitschriften," in *Rendering / Visualisierung* (Begriffe des digitalen Bildes, 5), ed. Hubert Locher, Dominik Lengyel, Florian Henrich, and Catherine Toulouse, Munich 2024, pp. 28–54. DOI: https://doi.org/10.5282/ubm/epub.109218

24 Cf. e.g. Heiko Haberle, "Sieben Architektur-Influencer und ihre Themen," in *DAB*, 25.2.2020, <https://www.dabonline.de/2020/02/25/architektur-fotos-influencer-baufluencer-architekten-bei-instagram-facebook-twitter/#comments> (last accessed 17.1.2024).

25 SR, "[Editorial]," in *Bauwelt*, 85, 1994, 20 (20 May), p. 1073.

26 Dietmar Steiner, "Wie die Bauwelt jetzt ist …," in *Bauwelt*, 101, 2010, 1/2 (8 Jan.), pp. 8–9, here p. 9.

manipulation in the course of its transformation into media form, is always a portrayal—even if, like it or not, a designed interpretation always remains[21]—the design as an imaginative anticipation of the future needs to be materialized in a medium. The representation, as a physical, photographed, or digital model, as a sketch, drawing, or rendering, is required to give form to an intention, to be able to develop, modify, and produce this intention, but also in order to present, market, and sell the project. Accordingly, a design visualization is always a communication of an architectural idea in the form of an image that was designed and created for this purpose.[22]

Design and visualization are linked through the image. The two analytically distinguishable areas interact with and influence each other directly or through the design as image products—which emerge in the example of Herzog & de Meuron in the design process, where they find application—as well as pictorial representations that are not infrequently created by external service providers for the purpose of communicating the design to the outside world and that currently circulate as image media in discussions of the architecture and in turn influence the design process.

Here it must be openly stated that this interaction is by no means a genuine digital phenomenon. Ever since architecture began to be communicated using media in professional practice, images as aesthetically created representations of a design in extremely multifarious forms have conveyed information through the available channels of distribution and reception; and, under these circumstances, the design team was always exposed to these communicative, informative, and inspirational forms of image. Also and especially, the designers receive these images, which then influence design practice and finally the completed building. Everything points to the fact that such influence through the image is becoming more intensive in both quantity and quality in the digital age. The field of design visualization is undergoing a dramatic upswing due to digitalization. Following the postmodern drawing boom, the emergence of computer-generated renderings results in a boom in architectural presentation images, which this project has investigated and evidenced based on, for example, the journals.[23] The digital architectural image's ease of availability and reproducibility, due to, for example, the speed and range of media distribution, has earned it the status of a global mass medium, one that is found everywhere and is present at all times. Social media channels such as Instagram play a considerable part, not only for the designers and visualizers but also as platforms and idea exchanges for other participants in the architectural process.[24] The rise of the rendering as the dominating image medium in architectural representation happened so swiftly that, by the middle of the 1990s, it is well on the "way to becoming the anonymous architecture image machine,"[25] while fifteen years later images would go on to gain "total mastery over architectural journalism."[26] This boom of the image in the course of digitalization is not without consequences for design, as the architectural photographer Jens Ludloff outlines in *Bauwelt* in 2012:

> "The present generation of students has […] a panoramic knowledge of images. On the other hand, most of them have never been to these places. Our knowledge of images is growing daily, but our 'knowledge of presence' is becoming ever less. […] If our

157

The Dialectic of the Digital Image in the Architectural Process

27 Nils Ballhausen in the interview with Jan Bitter and Jens Ludloff about architectural photography, in *Bauwelt*, 103, 2012, 25 (29 June), pp. 2–3, here p. 3.

28 See the contribution from Florian Henrich, Dominik Lengyel, and Catherine Toulouse, pp. 34–137.

29 Cf. the early, critical use in Heinrich Klotz, "Die Architekturzeichnung als Medium einer neuen Ästhetik," in *Jahrbuch für Architektur 1981/1982*, Braunschweig and Wiesbaden 1981, pp. 150–51, here p. 150.

30 Helge Bofinger, "Helmut Jacoby—Meister der Architekturzeichnung," in *Helmut Jacoby. Meister der Architekturzeichnung*, ed. Helge Bofinger and Wolfgang Voigt, exhib. cat., Tübingen 2001, pp. 8–13, here p. 11.

31 Cf. also Florian Henrich, "Das Analoge im Digitalen. Entwurfsvisualisierung zwischen Partizipation und Fotorealismus," in *Lens On. Fotografieren in architektonischen Entwurfsprozessen der Moderne*, ed. Tobias Becker, Teresa Fankhänel, Dennis Jelonnek, and Sarine Waltenspül, Berlin 2023, pp. 13–26.

32 See → Image 36, p. 106.

33 Hubertus Adam, "Nutzungsmischung Philharmonie," in *Bauwelt*, 99, 2008, 1/2 (4 Jan.), pp. 52–55, here p. 52.

competence in handling images continues to grow, perhaps soon we will have buildings that are built images. […] We have always designed with the help of images. […] When designing, we start with an image and transform the image into a three-dimensional space. The latter is eventually—perhaps—built, and then photographed, making it again a two-dimensional image. That is a quite normal procedure. The question is: Does the space change, if our knowledge of space relates overwhelmingly to our knowledge of images?"[27]

In addition to the quantitative dimension, the qualitative properties of the digital architectural image, the means by which it is designed and the aesthetic requirements, were also examined as part of the research project.[28] The success and mass distribution of the digital architectural image as the new standard of design staging has led once again in the history of architecture representation to the supremacy of the pictorial: there is a clearly visible tendency that moves away from the primacy of the abstraction of axonometric projection to a new vividness of the perspective, illusionistic, colorful, atmospherically suggestive, even the emotive or sentimental representation produced using the computer. The renewed upswing of the image takes place under the name of *photorealism*,[29] a term adopted from the paintings of the 1970s and a compositional mode that aims for the design to appear as the "anticipated photograph of the later building."[30] All the diversity of stylistic trends and currents generated by digital photorealism as the predominant image mode of design visualization in the last twenty years have one characteristic above all in common: a pictorial anticipation of the future in the mode of the photograph, and with that the concealment of the provisional status of the design as something possible that has still to be developed, modified, and designed.

This appears to us as important in two ways. Firstly, there is the principal, long-standing point of criticism of pictorial- or appearance-focused methods of representation that they induce viewers, including laypeople and in particular the client, to judge a design not in accordance with specific architectural aspects but rather from the impression of its pictorial reproduction. While the postmodern drawing boom, with its primacy of abstract axonometry up to the end of the 1980s, was increasingly criticized as being a "mystification of three-dimensionality" incapable of being understood by laypeople, and the design visualization generated by computer was welcomed as a factually concrete, natural "simulation" of the building in its built state, the pendulum has now swung in the opposite direction: with the photorealistic rendering, the architectural presentation image achieves a suggestive illusionism of a quality never seen before, which is sometimes heavily criticized.[31]

Secondly, through the suggestive quality of the photorealistic rendering in combination with its pervasiveness as a specific characteristic of the digital image, the fictive image of a design, and not just the picture of the completed building, has experienced an enormous increase in its potential as an influencing factor, model, and source of inspiration for future architecture. Hardly anything illustrates this more clearly than the Elbphilharmonie in Hamburg by Herzog & de Meuron.[32] This project showed that a "handful of visualizations" could contribute crucially to making "reality […] out of an idée fixe."[33] It can also be seen

Hubert Locher, Florian Henrich

Fig. 4, "Hey, I'm standing in the rendering!"—left: Rendering by Herzog & de Meuron for the development of Tacheles-Brache in Berlin, in *Bauwelt*, 2019, issue 23 (15 Nov.), p. 35, © Herzog & de Meuron; right: New builds on Riebeckplatz in Halle / Saale, fall 2021, photograph: © Florian Henrich

34 Andrea Roedig, "Hey, ich steh im Rendering! Über Architektur, Bild und Realismus," in *wespennest*, 2015, 169 (Nov.), pp. 66–69.

35 Sabine Ammon, "Epilog. Vom Siegeszug der Bildlichkeit im Zeitalter der Modellierung," in Ammon and Hinterwaldner, *Bildlichkeit im Zeitalter*, pp. 399–426.

36 Christophe Barlieb and Lidia Gasperoni, "Einleitung," in *Media Agency. Neue Ansätze zur Medialität in der Architektur*, ed. Christophe Barlieb and Lidia Gasperoni, Bielefeld 2020, pp. 7–11, here p. 8.

from this example that the selected form of visualization corresponded ideally with the type of architecture and the implied intended effects. While this building is intended to atmospherically and suggestively integrate into the Hamburg harbor landscape—graphically taking up the metaphor of the ship and by means of visual internal effects, such as the reflective surfaces and undulating edges, literally extending the metaphor—the design demands an appropriately realistic as well as fictional implementation in the architectural image. There is no question, it would certainly have been possible to prepare axonometric drawings for this design by digital means, but they would hardly have been able to unleash the same kind of effect. Indeed, other pictorial forms of design representation are capable of exercising such influence. One example would be Mies van der Rohe's charcoal drawings for the Berlin skyscraper competition in 1921, although Mies himself preferred to use photomontages, which anticipate the effect of the photorealistic rendering using analog means. With computer-generated photorealistic visualizations, their effect can be so far-reaching that they predetermine the view of built architecture in such a way that the viewer gets the impression, "Hey, I'm standing in the rendering!"[34] (Fig. 4)

It is clear here how photorealistic image elements of digital design visualizations can have an effect on the recipients—designers, users, and consumers: existing buildings, in this case recent new builds, are reminders of images seen somewhere before, be it in a journal, on a website, in an advertisement, on Instagram; the built becomes associated with the depicted, the real with the fictive. The focus is less on the question of whether the design representation appears deceivingly real and more on the impression that real architecture looks like images. Buildings until now never viewed are perceived as familiar because they already seem well-known from their images. Through photorealistic renderings, the pictorial representation of the design gains power to influence well before it is ever built, and fashions our ideas of future architecture and our perception of the built.

The way ahead

One important aim of the exemplary synopsis on the development of the digital architectural image in this book was to highlight the dialectic of design and visualization in the medium of the digital image. Further research remains to be done into the interactions with the actual built environment. Building on the knowledge obtained from this project, the next step in research would be to ask what influence more recent digital design methods have on the achieved result, how is the detected "triumphal procession of imagery"[35] to be seen in relation to the similarly detected "crisis of representation"[36] in the field of digital design, whether a reciprocal or a dialectic relationship can be assumed here, and what consequences for the architectural form emerge out of that relationship.

Likewise, research could be continued into the digital image as a medium of architectural representation from 1980 to today to observe the current situation more intensively and move the focus onto image practice in professional architectural design offices, on its actual use

160

Hubert Locher, Florian Henrich

37 Cf. as a point of connection Beatriz Colomina, *Privacy and Publicity: Modern Architecture as Mass Media*, Cambridge (Mass.) 1994.

and the various groups of actors involved, on media channels and commercial structures.

Finally, on the same basis, the question of the global dimension of the digital image in architecture: New builds in Oslo today are similar to those in Berlin or Detroit. An empty sense of vague déjà vu descends, a feeling that these or similar buildings have been seen before. Has the digitalization of design visualization led to a homogenization of architectural representation? Or could it even be that globalization of digital architectural representation has contributed to the genesis of a homogeneous contemporary "building style"? Exploring these lines of thought a little further, it could be said that this form of new "international style" cannot be traced back solely to the influence of digital design tools but is more likely to be the result of the omnipresence in the media of images of more or less the same type. Architecture in the digital age appears in this observation above all as a pictorial phenomenon and thus demands to be recorded and understood as such.[37]

161

The Dialectic of the Digital Image in the Architectural Process

Hubert Locher,
Dominik Lengyel,
Florian Henrich,
Catherine Toulouse

Architecture Transformed— Ten Theses on the Digital Architectural Image

1   In their anthology *Bildlichkeit im Zeitalter der Modellierung*, Sabine Ammon and Inge Hinterwaldner define the "sphere of interaction between representativeness (imaging something) and productivity (enabling something)" in digital design processes, and explore the "interplay between vividness and functionality, pictoriality and a model-like nature." Inge Hinterwaldner, "Prolog. Modellhaftigkeit und Bildlichkeit in Entwurfsartefakten," in *Bildlichkeit im Zeitalter der Modellierung. Operative Artefakte in Entwurfsprozessen der Architektur und des Ingenieurwesens*, ed. Sabine Ammon and Inge Hinterwaldner, Munich 2017, pp. 13–30, here p. 13.

First: Our project starts with the acceptance of the principle of architecture, which can be traced back to the beginnings of the discourse on architectural theory, to Vitruvius's *The Ten Books on Architecture*. The author offers the opinion that architectural knowledge (*scientia*) grows from practice and exercise (*fabrica*) as well as from intellectual work (*raciocinatio*) (I, Ch. I, 2). From this we draw the conclusion that the concept of architecture requires a wider view of practical and creative work as well as critical reflection as a form of visual thinking in the overall view of many different individual themes. Both perspectives feature in our project. Both dimensions come together in the visible image of the projected architecture. The digital image created using software is its contemporary form.

Second: In accordance with the above fundamental acceptance of principle, the concept of architecture, in the way we treat it here, requires the consideration of its processuality. In our opinion, the image plays a key function in the architectural realization process: it offers the possibility to show something that can be imagined but does not yet exist. It relates to reality, anticipates however prospectively the yet to be realized, connects theoretical and practical knowledge, while accepting the risk that the presently untried is a projection. The image is therefore both a depiction and a model at the same time.[1] The available digital tools for creating image models and model images reinforce this dual direction of the image in a specific way.

Third: This dual orientation applies to every architectural image used in the architectural process. However, it is still possible to differentiate between various functions. The diagram, design sketch, and hand drawing are used during the design process in various phases. The principle of this image form in the design process is abstraction, provisionality, incompleteness, in other words an openness for further creativity or a pause for curtailment and decisions over changes in direction. At the other end of the process or in one of its iterative loops stands the visualization as an adequately concretized conceptual model that borders on the fictional portrayal of the future state and is often confused with it. From this idealized typical split emerges a bifurcation of the architectural image into design and visualization, which can be traced as a division of this specialized work back into the eighteenth century.

Fourth: The principal differences between the digital image in the separate contexts of design and visualization continued while digitalization progressed. *Modeling*, the creation of the digital geometric model as a main constituent of design, provides the structure, ahead of *Rendering*, the creative pictorial elaboration of the model using the computer. Strictly speaking, rendering is not a design tool; it is a subsequent part of the design process. Designing takes place first, with and on the model. Rendering sets the design *in scene* as an image using an appropriate choice of visualization and image processing software. As a pictorial representation of the design, rendering is intended to visually anticipate the future state of a completed building and by these means communicate the fundamental idea. As such, it fulfills the purpose not of a production tool but rather of a communicative function between mediation and marketing primarily directed outward beyond the design process, whether it be used for presentation, in a competition, or for marketing, advertising, or sales. The two-part nature of the digital

Architecture Transformed—Ten Theses on the Digital Architectural Image architectural image manifests itself technically as a hiatus in the development of digital tools: the computer was first used to assist in design and only later for its visualization. The time delay for this in the journals is around ten years. For a long time, the computer was used far more for realizing buildings than graphically depicting them.

Fifth: What can be observed from a general view on the screens of digital interfaces over the last four decades also applies in a special way to the field of architecture. As the use of computer technology increases, it is accompanied by a continual and in the end almost exponential upsurge in the importance of imagery in the design process and in architecture in general. The visual and visualization become a constitutive component. Correspondingly, a growing penetration of the sphere of the design image (modeling) takes place with those types of communication image (rendering). Designers make increasing use of pictorial computer visualization in order to—as was done in earlier times with the endoscope or the video camera—place themselves into the design and assess it in preparation for the next step of coming out of the illusion again and performing the necessary changes on the design model.

Sixth: This observation of a growing tendency to include more or less illusionistic or artistic images in the design process corresponds with the assumption of two different modes of imagery, operative and representative imagery, which engage with one another in a more or less fluid alternation of abstraction and immersion. Even if design and visualization are two different processes in which different forms of digital images are created, we should not see them as standing in opposition to one another but as being in a relationship of mutual influence. Even those images that were not created for use solely within the design team are part of the current architectural discourse in which the designers participate as well. They are involved as received media artifacts in the architectural image memory of the participating actors and influence their imaginations—with manifest or latent results—as a reference, inspiration, or model in the design process. With the digitalization of the image and the medium used for its distribution, this reciprocal relationship between design and visualization has achieved a global currency.

Seventh: A look at digital design tools reveals significant image-based and visually communicated differences. It is not only operative and representative imagery that are heavily enmeshed with each other. The entire process of design on a performative level moves from a highly cognitively conditioned process that assumes an above-average ability to think in three dimensions toward a less abstract, more intuitive, creative, and graphical design: from design in plan, elevation, and section toward design in multiple perspectives. The image does not only represent the finished product or an intermediate stage in its creation but rather behaves as a transformative, operative medium providing continuous support for the whole duration of the design process.

Eighth: From the mid-2000s, rendering—a computer-based visualization technique using a versatile range of creative frame surface coverings with a tendency toward providing illusionistic representations—achieved domination of design visualization as an image medium and by and large replaced the analog and hybrid processes generally in use up to that time. In terms of creativity, it proved to be more focused on purpose and less on innovation. On the one hand, the paradigm of

164

Hubert Locher, Dominik Lengyel, Florian Henrich, Catherine Toulouse photorealism—the visual anticipation of the future in the form of a photograph and with that the concealment of the provisional character of the representation—has enjoyed an unbroken reign. On the other, the main and very often emphasized aspect of the atmospheric: the addition of an aesthetic added value by the use of compositional means is designed to have a suggestive effect and takes into account the communicative function of these images. At the same time, this is characteristic of their photorealism, as they are not simply intended to depict the design realistically, but to present it in the most favorable light possible by means of pictorial staging that goes beyond the purely architectural, thus aesthetically exaggerating the depicted reality. However, alongside the increasing criticism of digital photorealism, a significant return to alternative digital approaches to image design is observed from the mid-2010s, in particular an increasing focus on analog graphical processes.

Ninth: There has hardly been any notable engagement with the digital image as a medium of architectural representation, let alone a critical, reflective analysis. While digital design tools continue to be covered in teaching establishments, the topic of rendering has hardly entered the architectural discourse to this day. Although this form of digital architectural image can be found practically everywhere in our everyday lives, its aesthetic and pictorial qualities for the most part remain unnoticed. This invisibility in the discourse over architecture is characteristic: the ultimate aim of the seemingly final visualization of the design by means of photorealistic rendering is the deceptive fiction, the quasi-photographic representation. If this aim is achieved, the image is taken for the reality of the fiction.

Tenth: In the digital age, a criticism of the digital image in its various forms of appearance is essential so that its creative design potential and its power to influence can be adequately described and used in the architectural process. The reason for this is the ever-increasing importance of the image as an interface between humans and machine.

165

The Authors

Hubert Locher
Professor of History and Theory of Visual Media at the Philipps
University of Marburg and Director of the German Documentation
Center for Art History (DDK-Bildarchiv Foto Marburg)

Dominik Lengyel
Professor of Architecture and Visualization at Brandenburg
University of Technology Cottbus-Senftenberg and Founding
Partner at Lengyel Toulouse Architects

Florian Henrich
M.A., Research Associate at the German Documentation Center for
Art History (DDK-Bildarchiv Foto Marburg)

Catherine Toulouse
Academic Assistant to the Chair of Architecture and Visualization
at Brandenburg University of Technology Cottbus-Senftenberg and
Founding Partner at Lengyel Toulouse Architects

Imprint

Hubert Locher, Dominik Lengyel, Florian Henrich, Catherine Toulouse

This book is a result of the research project "Architecture Transformed—Architectural Processes in the Digital Image Space" as part of the DFG Priority Program "The Digital Image" 2172.

Published with the support of the DFG, the German Documentation Center for Art History—Bildarchiv Foto Marburg, Philipps-Universität Marburg.

Content and Production Editor: Katharina Holas, Angelika Gaal, Birkhäuser Verlag, Vienna, Austria
Translation from German into English: Raymond Peat, Alford, UK
Proofreading: John Sweet, Montréal, Canada
Layout, cover design, and typography: Floyd E. Schulze, Birkhäuser Verlag, Berlin, Germany
Image editing: Pixelstorm Litho & Digital Imaging, Vienna, Austria
Printing: Beltz Grafische Betriebe GmbH, Bad Langensalza, Germany
Paper: Magno Volume 150 gsm
Typeface: LL Circular

Library of Congress Control Number: 2024932913

Bibliographic information published by the German National Library
The German National Library lists this publication in the Deutsche Nationalbibliografie; detailed bibliographic data are available on the Internet at http://dnb.dnb.de.

ISBN 978-3-0356-2448-9
e-ISBN (PDF) 978-3-0356-2877-7

© 2024 Birkhäuser Verlag GmbH, Basel
Im Westfeld 8, 4055 Basel, Switzerland
Part of Walter de Gruyter GmbH, Berlin/Boston

9 8 7 6 5 4 3 2 1   www.birkhauser.com